YOUR
TWIN
FLAME
JOURNEY

YOUR TWIN FLAME JOURNEY

A guide to understanding your soul's most passionate connection

THERESA CHEUNG

GODSFIELD

First published in Great Britain in 2026 by Godsfield Press, an imprint of
Octopus Publishing Group Ltd
Carmelite House
50 Victoria Embankment
London EC4Y 0DZ
www.octopusbooks.co.uk

An Hachette UK Company
www.hachette.co.uk

The authorized representative in the EEA is Hachette Ireland,
8 Castlecourt Centre, Dublin 15, D15 XTP3, Ireland (email: info@hbgi.ie)

Text copyright © Theresa Cheung 2025

Distributed in the US by Hachette Book Group
1290 Avenue of the Americas, 4th and 5th Floors
New York, NY 10104

Distributed in Canada by Canadian Manda Group
664 Annette St., Toronto, Ontario, Canada M6S 2C8

All rights reserved. No part of this work may be reproduced or utilized in
any form or by any means, electronic or mechanical, including photocopying,
recording or by any information storage and retrieval system,
without the prior written permission of the publisher.

Theresa Cheung asserts the right to be identified as the author of this work.

ISBN 978-1-84181-633-3
eBook ISBN 978-1-84181-635-7

A CIP catalogue record for this book is available from the British Library.

Typeset in 11.25/17 pt Heldane Text by Six Red Marbles UK, Thetford, Norfolk

Printed and bound in Great Britain.

13 5 7 9 10 8 6 4 2

Commissioning Editor: Louisa Johnson
Project Editor: Rimsha Falak
Copy Editor: Monica Hope
Creative Director: Mel Four
Production Controller: Sarah Parry

This FSC® label means that materials used for
the product have been responsibly sourced.

iStock: Anastasiia_M 169, 170, 171, 172; Andrii Moroziuk 55;
ChrisGorgio 140; Grace Maina 51; Magnilion 54; PeterHermesFurian 52, 143–165;
Pamela Colman Smith, public domain, via Wikimedia Commons 185

For all who long for a higher love

Contents

Introduction: It's Your Love Story	1
Chapter One: The Heart of the Matter	23
Chapter Two: Karmic Bonds, False Flames and Soul Mates	61
Chapter Three: Twin Flames Signs and Stages	103
Chapter Four: Twin Flame Astrology	137
Chapter Five: Dreamwork and the Twin Flame Journey	199
Chapter Six: Unrequited Love	219
Chapter Seven: Twin Flame Union and Your Awakened Psychic Abilities	251
Conclusion: Higher Love	277
Source Notes	291
Acknowledgements	293
About the Author	295
Index	297

Introduction

IT'S YOUR LOVE STORY

And so, it begins.

You might not yet fully realize it, but by choosing to open your heart and mind to the words in this book, you are stepping into the most profound love story you'll ever experience – the story of *you* and your Twin Flame.

This path you are about to walk is one that will feel both strangely familiar and startlingly new, deeply comforting yet often uncomfortable, exhilarating and challenging in equal measure. It will take you to places you never imagined and transform you in ways you never thought possible. Yet, as unexpected as this path may be, it is the only one that can lead you to feelings of wholeness and the higher love you've always yearned for.

If, in this moment, you commit to fully embracing the higher love and truth that awaits you within these pages – if you allow yourself to absorb the wisdom, the revelations and the insights into who you are and the destiny of your relationships – you will find yourself on the brink of a whole new world.

This is not merely a journey – it's the start of a deep and transformative personal and spiritual awakening. As you turn each page, you'll connect with the powerful energy of Twin Flame love, awakening a strength within you that will never fade. By the time you reach the final pages, your heart will be filled with an unshakable, radiant force, forever changed by its promise and joy.

This is your great Cosmic Love story. And it begins here and now.

Do Twin Flames Really Exist?

But does your Twin Flame – your other half, the one who is made for you, 'completes' you and loves everything about you – really exist? And if they do, will you ever get to celebrate one fine Valentine's Day with them in a moment of destiny that feels like it was written in the stars?

The concept of Twin Flames (or Divine Unions, Spiritual Mirrors, Cosmic Love) often sounds like a lofty, romantic ideal – an impossible dream, a fairytale, something that belongs in movies or novels. It begs several questions. Is there someone out there who is made for you and only you? Someone whose heart will resonate perfectly with yours and who is waiting for you to find them? And is it simply a matter of doing whatever it takes to find and meet them? What if the person who is *meant* for you – the one who will bring you the deepest sense of fulfilment – is someone you've never met, someone you've never seen, someone you don't even know exists?

Someone to Complete You?

This is the big question posed by Annie (Meg Ryan) in the classic 1993 romcom *Sleepless in Seattle* as she stands on the cusp of a major life decision. The notion that true love will transcend comfort and security to pursue something deeper is at the heart of the Twin Flame Journey. In a dramatic Valentine's Day moment, Annie leaves her safe, secure fiancé Walter, who she has been with for years, to pursue a connection with Sam (Tom Hanks) – a man she has only heard on the radio but never met in person. Despite the risks and after a little low-key stalking, Annie refuses to settle for 'good enough'. She breaks free from her old life and follows the spark of electric, undeniable chemistry with Sam.

For Walter, Annie's decision is devastating, but there's a twist: perhaps, in his own Twin Flame Path, he has dodged a bullet. He is now free to find someone *made* for him, as Annie clearly wasn't his perfect match. In this light, he too might be walking the path to his true Spiritual Mirror – someone whose energy will match his own.

Similarly, in the 1996 iconic romantic movie *Jerry Maguire*, when Tom Cruise's character, Jerry, tells Renée Zellweger's Dorothy, 'You complete me,' it feels like the pinnacle of romantic expression. But can this idea of being 'completed' by another person be misguided? Jerry's declaration seems a little one-sided. Dorothy has sacrificed so much for Jerry's happiness throughout the movie, giving up parts of herself in the process. After their 'happily ever after', it's easy to wonder whether Dorothy will ever look back and question where her own desires and identity went.

The Romance of Twin Flames in Pop Culture

Romcoms have a special place in our hearts. We adore how they tell us that true love will always find a way. The longing, the passion, the bliss, the heartbreak, the union – they invite us to vicariously experience every twist and turn of the romantic journey. Whether it's *Sleepless in Seattle*, *Jerry Maguire*, *Serendipity*, *Notting Hill*, *The Notebook*, *Brokeback Mountain*, or *Bridget Jones's Diary*, we get to dream along with the characters, cheering them on as they chase the love they crave.

But these films, as beloved as they are for their 'feel-good' escapism, often fail to show us the full picture of Twin Flame love. They typically depict the early stages of love, the first sparks that ignite between two people, but don't delve into the real work that happens after the honeymoon phase. These stories rarely show us the growing pains, the learning and the transformation that occur in a true, lasting relationship. For Cosmic Love to flourish, it requires much more than chemistry – it needs two people to consciously evolve together, with a commitment to a higher form of love.

Literature too has long explored the idea of Divine Union, of two souls destined to be together. From Shakespeare's *Romeo and Juliet* and its star-crossed lovers to the telepathic bond between Jane and Rochester in *Jane Eyre*, the seeds of Twin Flame energy can be seen in many classic tales. In *Pride and Prejudice*, Elizabeth and Darcy undergo a slow-burning transformation towards each other, recognizing the deeper truth of their connection. The passionate, magnetic pull between the Duke and Daphne in *Bridgerton*, or the forbidden love of Evelyn Hugo in *The Seven Husbands of*

Evelyn Hugo, or that intense 'I see you' passion between Cathy and Heathcliff in *Wuthering Heights* echo the timeless story of two souls destined to both reflect and reveal each other.

These iconic stories are captivating, but they are still just that: stories. They are a lens through which we view love, but they often create misconceptions about what real Twin Flame connection is. Crucially, these fictional tales rarely touch on the most important and unacknowledged part of the journey. Before you can attract your true Twin Flame, you must first develop a fulfilling relationship with yourself.

Self-Love, Actually

The reality is, to align with your perfect match you must first be aligned with yourself. It's a truth that often feels counterintuitive. When you're yearning for that perfect Soul Mate, the idea that you need first to focus on self-love may feel like an unwelcome distraction and redirection. But this is where the Twin Flame Journey really begins. Until you can fill your own inner void – until you can recognize and nurture your own worth – any romantic relationship you enter will be incomplete, misaligned, or unfulfilling.

This is why, throughout this book, we will focus on more than just guiding you towards finding your Twin Flame. We will also explore the deeper, more transformative work of cultivating the most essential relationship in your life: the one you have with yourself. It's only by nurturing self-love that you can truly attract Cosmic Love.

Balancing Self-Love with Love for Others

This is not to say that your Twin Flame – the one who can truly 'see you' and who will resonate with your soul on a profound level – isn't out there somewhere in time waiting for you. Far from it! Your Spiritual Mirror is out there, but the key to meeting them lies in your ability to simultaneously grow your relationship with yourself while remaining open to the possibility of a powerful authentic connection with another person. The Twin Flame Journey is not a passive one. It's a proactive process that involves both self-discovery and the humility to remain open to others.

Self-love and an open mind and heart are the magnetic forces that draw your perfect match into your life. When you align with your highest self and cultivate love from within, you start vibrating at a frequency that naturally attracts your Twin Flame. It's a delicate balancing act. But it's worth it. When you learn to love yourself deeply and authentically, you are not only on your Twin Flame Voyage – you are walking towards a higher love, one that transcends the romanticized ideal and blossoms into a soul-affirming connection. And when the time is right, you will know. The love you have and the love you share will no longer be the stuff of fairytales – it will be real, grounded and deeply fulfilling. This is the power, the passion and the promise of Divine Union.

Your First Heart Stop

As you awaken to the importance of tuning in to the voice of your own heart, you are now ready to face one of the first significant milestones and the first heart stop on your Twin Flame Journey: Valentine's Day.

But what does Valentine's Day truly mean to you? If you could capture your feelings about Valentine's Day in just a few words, what would they be? Pause for a moment, place your hand over your heart and listen intently to what it is trying to tell you. If you can, write down what you sense. Afterwards, be sure to keep your note somewhere safe, because later in your journey, as you continue to walk the path of self-discovery and spiritual awakening, it will be enlightening to return to those words and reflect on how your perspective has evolved.

For now, though, let's stay present.

Does Valentine's Day fill you with joy, passion and romantic longing? Or does it stir feelings of dread, sadness, or nostalgia? Perhaps it's anger, disappointment, despondency, regret, guilt, anxiety, or even loneliness that arises when you think of this day?

There is no 'right' or 'wrong' response here. Your feelings are valid, whatever they may be. Write them down honestly, without judgment or expectation. Even if your emotions are contradictory or don't seem to make sense, trust that your heart knows the truth. Remember, this is for your eyes only, so allow yourself the space to be open and authentic.

Your current feelings about Valentine's Day matter because they are the launch point of your Twin Flame Awakening. They indicate where you stand emotionally and energetically and will likely point you towards the loving direction you need to take.

As discussed below, it is entirely possible that your perspective on this most romantic day of the year needs to be recalibrated. You may find it necessary to free yourself from the expectations, traditions and narratives that have been imposed on you. Only then can the wisdom of your heart emerge and rescript your understanding of true love and authentic ways to celebrate it.

The Valentine's Day Paradox

Whether you love it or loathe it, Valentine's Day is inescapable in Western culture. Like taxes, it comes around with unyielding predictability. For some, Valentine's Day may arrive with a sense of enchantment; and for others, it's nothing short of a cringeworthy reminder of unattainable ideals.

Everywhere you look – on TV screens, in store windows, online stores – it's the same image: heart-shaped chocolates, hot-pink balloons and an endless supply of gift cards filled with messages of undying love. There are rose-petal trails, candlelit dinners and packed restaurants teeming with hand-holding couples. Social media becomes a parade of romantic stories, videos and images that paint the picture of perfect love. It's almost impossible to avoid the weight of these representations, especially if your own love life doesn't match the idealized narrative.

If you are single, these portrayals may leave you feeling unlovable, as though your worth is somehow less because you're not 'coupled up' on this day. Even if you cherish your independence, the overwhelming Western cultural message of Valentine's Day can still spark feelings of inadequacy. If you're in a relationship, perhaps the day brings the pressure of unspoken expectations – pressure to 'perform' or to somehow fulfil a vision of romance that may not reflect your reality. Tensions may surface. Arguments may arise. The desire to meet external standards could prompt overspending on gifts or cards, leaving you with a sense of emptiness despite your best intentions.

The truth is, behind the rose-tinted glasses, Valentine's Day can be highly paradoxical. A day meant to celebrate the joy of romantic love often stirs up pain, loneliness and even resentment. Break-ups tend to peak around 14 February, as unmet expectations and hurt feelings boil to the surface. For example, *Psychology Today* reported that 'partners in romantic relationships already in a weakened state were almost five times more likely to break up within the two weeks surrounding Valentine's Day than they were during any other weeks of the year'.[1] It's as if a day intended to elevate the heart can instead drag it down. But then, when we look more deeply, we see how this energetic dissonance may well be rooted in the history of the day itself.

Tainted Love

Valentine's Day has a long, complicated history, one that is far from the romanticized version we know today. Its origins trace back to Ancient Roman rituals – including brutal sacrifices and executions. In the third century, Emperor Claudius II executed two men, both of whom happened to be named Valentine, on 14 February (in different years), which resonates with the darker, more violent origins of the holiday.[2] The celebration itself was later co-opted by the Church, blending it with a pagan fertility festival. It wasn't until the Renaissance and the Shakespearean era that Valentine's Day began to take on a more romanticized tone.

The modern, commercialized version that fills our shop and online windows emerged during the Industrial Revolution, with Hallmark cards taking charge in the early 20th century. From that moment onwards, 14 February transformed into an annual display of romantic consumerism and billions are now spent every year in the name of love. So, here's the truth you have probably intuitively known all along: Valentine's Day is a business. It is a manufactured experience that uses romantic love as a hook with the purpose of generating revenue.

Valentine's Day-Proofing Your Heart

Now that you see this day for what it truly is – a mixture of cultural conditioning, marketing and idealized notions of romance – you are free to reclaim your heart from its grip. This book aims to Valentine's Day-proof you forever. As you progress along your Twin Flame Path, you will come to realize that this day, with all its external pressures and expectations, has no power over your relationship with true love.

Valentine's Day will simply become another checkpoint in your journey, a moment to reflect on the next loving step you are taking on your Twin Flame Journey. It will no longer dictate your emotional state, control your mind or heart, or pressure your bank account. Whether you choose to celebrate it, ignore it, or treat it like any other day, you will be anchored in the truth that love – the forever kind – flows from within you and does not require external validation.

In the end, you will come to see that the greatest and most loving gift you can give yourself on Valentine's Day – or any day – is the freedom to define love on your own terms. Your own heart's wisdom will guide you to a love that is authentic, unwavering and beyond the constraints of societal expectations.

A Life of Love and Lessons, So Far . . .

Before we embark together on your great love-story adventure in search of your Divine Union, I feel it's important to share my own credentials. What qualifies me to guide you through the relationship signposts, the soul-deep teachings and the lessons of love you will encounter on your own path?

Well, aside from the simple fact that I am a human being with a heart that beats and loves to love – just like you – I have spent my entire life researching, studying and writing about personal and spiritual growth. I've dedicated my writing career to helping others navigate the complexities of self-awareness, love and the mysteries of the soul. And here's the truth I've consistently discovered and taught along the way: meaningful personal and spiritual growth cannot happen in isolation. Relationships are where the real transformation takes place. They are the school where we learn, grow and evolve. It is in our interactions with others that we walk our deepest truths and do the real work of understanding and finding love.

I'd like you from now on to think of your relationships as your higher-love school. They hold the power to increase your self-worth, offer you self-understanding and create opportunities for connection and spiritual awakening. They mirror aspects of your own personality, exposing parts of you that are repressed or denied, or trauma that needs to be released. They invite you to heal and become more self-aware, develop empathy and discover your deepest needs. But just as relationships have the power to illuminate, they also can dim and distort. Relationships that are not aligned with your highest good can pull you off course, disempowering you and veering you far from your one true Twin Flame Path.

I believe this book is something I was meant to write – though I now know it wasn't meant to be born until my later years. One of the gifts of ageing is the luxury of hindsight, the opportunity to see with greater clarity the lessons every relationship in my life has imparted.

Like most of us, I am still a work in progress. But each day, I move closer to a higher love. My own Twin Flame Journey is rich with meaning, adventure and purpose. I can feel it unfolding as I learn and grow. But that path to acceptance and celebration hasn't been without its challenges. Along the way, I've encountered several intense relationships and had my fair share of heartbreaks, but I have absolute faith that my Twin Flame exists. I believe, in time, I will meet them. It might be in this lifetime, or it might be in another. They may appear romantically or in a platonic relationship. Or perhaps, they will reveal themselves in the most profound way: within myself. For now, I am content on my journey towards ever-increasing and fulfilling self-awareness and self-love. I don't feel incomplete. On the contrary, I feel liberated and blissful, excited to live and love again each new day. In essence, I am now at a stage in life when I am truly living and loving every single precious moment of my Twin Flame Adventure.

As I navigate my life, I'm not so concerned with *who, when,* or *where* my Spiritual Mirror will show up. Instead, I am focused on embracing the journey, trusting the process and loving the path. I believe this personal and spiritual unfolding – the one that brings me closer to a higher love – is more than enough. It is bliss.

Your Life of Love and Lessons, So Far...

And so, beloved reader, this is the essence of the journey you are about to embark on. No matter where you are in life – regardless of your age, relationship status, or the stage of your personal evolution – the path of the Twin Flame is about learning to fall in love with the adventure of your own life itself. It's about embracing every twist, every turn and every unexpected revelation as part of your unique journey. Through this process, you will not only learn to love yourself more deeply but also come into alignment with the divine love in your heart that is patiently waiting to reunite you with your Twin Flame. This union will heal and complete you in ways you never imagined.

And if, at any moment, you feel that time has passed for you to experience a higher love, that you are 'too old' or that it's too late, let me assure you – nothing could be further from the truth. You are never too old for Divine Union. However, you are too old to continue repeating the same patterns and mistakes in love. The chapters ahead will help you shed those old ways and open you to the unconditional love that awaits and is eagerly longing for you. Keep reading, for the best is yet to come.

What Lies Ahead

This book has been born from a multitude of questions that have come my way over the decades – from my readers, listeners of my *White Shores* podcast and my weekly UK

Health Radio show, and from people seeking clarity on their romantic journeys. They've asked me how to make sense of love from a spiritual perspective, how to attract it, how to heal broken hearts and how to recognize if they're headed in the right direction. This is not just a book; it is a response. A response written from the depths of my heart. It is my firm belief that its words will magnetically draw in the hearts of those destined to receive them. I do feel that nothing in this life is random and that you were meant to read or listen to it.

When you close the final page of this book, I hope you will feel as though you've read a love letter from your Twin Flame. I am certain that you will have found the answers you've longed for – and with them, the feelings of love, bliss and wholeness that your heart and soul have been yearning for.

In the chapters that follow, you will dive into the world of Karmic relationships, False Flames and Soul Mates. You will learn how these intimate relationships differ, how they serve as tools for personal growth and how, ultimately, they can all lead you back to the path towards your Twin Flame. Karmic and Soul Mate relationships are stepping stones for your personal growth, while your Twin Flame is the very catalyst that ignites your psychic and spiritual awakening. But do not mistake this for a hierarchy; all relationships – Karmic, Soul Mate and Twin Flame – serve one another. They are necessary to your evolution. Each one brings you wisdom, growth and a more intense, richer understanding of love, revealing the hidden desires of your heart. Personal growth cannot exist without spiritual growth, and vice versa; they are two sides of the same coin.

You may need to kiss a few Karmic frogs. You may need to seek comfort and healing in a Soul Mate (or two, or more), face your shadow through frustrating False Flame relationships and discover your own capacity for self-love. All of this is part of the process. To risk repeating myself, because it is so important, before you can fully enter into a Divine Union, you must first cultivate self-awareness, self-love and the hand-on-heart ability to stand on your own two feet. Until you are content in your own company, you cannot expect true fulfilment in a relationship. Personal growth through Karmic and Soul Mate relationships is essential for the spiritual awakening that marks the Divine Union. The journey is long and winding, but each relationship – each experience – is a necessary step on the path to becoming whole.

To maximize the impact of this book, I urge you to approach each chapter with mindfulness. Take your time. Reflect. As you progress, give yourself space to breathe, to check in with your heart and to allow the wisdom here to settle within. You will find exercises and rituals interspersed throughout the text – do not wait until the end to begin them. Do them as you go along. There is no value in overthinking the guidance you receive; the key to growth is in *living* the lessons, not just theorizing them. Walk the talk, and let the teachings guide you to speak and live your truth in the real world of love, dating, sex, marriage and beyond.

Here's what you can expect:

Chapter One: The Heart of the Matter. We will continue to unravel the mysteries surrounding the term 'Twin Flame' and dispel the misconceptions that cloud its meaning. You will gain insight into the origin, history and philosophy of

Twin Flames, as well as what science and psychology reveal about the wisdom of your heart.

Chapter Two: Karmic Bonds, False Flames and Soul Mates. We will navigate the world of Soul Mates and Karmic relationships, revealing how they differ from Twin Flames. These relationships are stepping stones – necessary for your personal growth. You will also explore the world of False Flame relationships, shedding light on how they reflect your shadow and how online love scams have intensified these heartaches.

Chapter Three: Twin Flame Signs and Stages. This chapter will investigate the signs that indicate you've met or are about to meet your Spiritual Mirror. You'll uncover the typical stages of a Twin Flame relationship, from the initial meeting to the stage of spiritual Ascension – liberation from external dependencies and connection to a higher power.

Chapter Four: Twin Flame Astrology. Here, you will discover how astrology can serve as a powerful tool for personal growth on your Twin Flame Path. Your birth chart holds the keys to understanding your love lessons and can guide you towards your true love direction. We will also explore other divination tools that can enhance your journey.

Chapter Five: Love Dreaming. Dreams offer insight into your Twin Flame Journey. This chapter will show you how to interpret your dreams as reflections of your progress and how you can use dream incubation to gain deeper understanding of your relationships and yourself.

Chapter Six: Unrequited Love. Self-love is the cornerstone of attracting your Twin Flame. This chapter will teach you how to begin loving yourself authentically and then guide you through the pain of unreturned love, helping you to transform it into self-healing and bliss. You'll also explore what it truly means to 'work' on a relationship – and when to let go if a relationship no longer aligns with your Twin Flame Path.

Chapter Seven: Twin Flame Union and Psychic Abilities. The journey to Divine Union awakens your innate psychic abilities. This chapter will help you harness and develop these gifts and show you how psychic activation can occur when your Twin Flame enters or exits your life. It will close with more heart-centred exercises and affirmations designed to awaken your psychic gifts and prepare you for higher love and spiritual Ascension.

Conclusion: Your Higher Love. The conclusion offers a renewed summary of the key teachings from the book, providing you with a practical guide to understanding the manifestation of Divine Union in your life. A word of caution, however: do not rush to this final section before you've fully absorbed the earlier chapters. Understanding the 'ending' before you experience the journey will only rob you of the transformative growth that happens along the way.

This is not just a book. It is a guide, a map, a treasure chest filled with wisdom meant to light your path. Embrace the journey – take it one chapter at a time. Your higher love is waiting, but you must first walk the path and experience the unexpected adventure along the way. The answers are already within you, and this book will help you remember things that should never have been forgotten.

Love Changes Everything

Twin Flame or higher love is not a quick fix, an easy solution, or something you simply claim as a prize. Instead, much like life itself, it is a journey, a continual unfolding, that deepens and expands along the way. Even when you think you have reached your destination and found the person of your 'dreams', I must tell you – there is no final point. The journey of spiralling ever higher into the infinite possibilities of Twin Flame love can never truly end.

Perhaps you're single, seeking your Spiritual Mirror. Or maybe you're already in a relationship and wondering, 'Is this the one?' Perhaps you've already met your Twin Flame but lost them – perhaps through grief or separation; or maybe, for complicated reasons, they can live only in your heart, not your life. Or you might be experiencing the arrow of unrequited love. Or perhaps you are content living solo and wondering if you're missing out.

No matter why you are here, I am deeply grateful that you are. I want this book to offer you reassurance: your Twin Flame Journey – and the higher love you are seeking, which is also always seeking you – is forever relevant. The longing you feel for the comfort and healing, and bliss of unconditional love is universal. There is nothing wrong with that yearning. What truly matters is how you respond to the eternal call of your heart, for it is your response that will change everything.

There is no better time than right now to lighten your emotional load, creating space for new learning, healing and growth to take root in your heart and mind. Now is the perfect time to release unrealistic romantic expectations and boldly take those first steps on your Twin Flame Journey. A journey that was quietly and magically laid before you the moment you opened these pages. All that remains now is for you to trust and follow it.

So, with these initial reflections and incentives complete, and as you officially begin your journey towards blissful higher love, take a deep, heart-centred breath. Then, with openness and purpose, turn the next page. It's high time to orient yourself, to walk with intention now and begin your utterly unique and always spellbinding Twin Flame Evolution.

Note: If, after reading this book, you feel called to reach out – to share your Cosmic Love stories, insights, or to ask any questions – please do. I'd love to hear from you. You can find my contact details in the 'About the Author' section at the end of this book. While my inbox may occasionally get busy (especially around Valentine's Day), I promise to make every effort to respond in due course. Thank you for your patience, and I look forward to connecting with you.

If you're suffering from a broken heart, feeling intensely lonely, or grieving the loss of a beloved companion, then – in addition to the advice in this book – please do seek out counselling, therapy, or the advice of your GP.

LIVING AND LOVING YOUR TWIN FLAME JOURNEY

'I am my beloved and my beloved is mine.'
Song of Solomon 6:3

1

THE HEART OF THE MATTER

Your heart will skip a beat, your head will spin, and your body will tingle all over when you first meet your Twin Flame. It's as if you've stumbled upon a story from a fairytale, or perhaps a dream that feels too real to wake up from. The sensation is at once electric and deeply familiar – a pull, a connection, a recognition that defies all logic. In their presence, you feel *known* in a way you've never experienced before. Seen. Accepted. Affirmed.

This is not fantasy; this is a recognition of the magic of unconditional love in its truest and highest form. A love that flows from a profound spiritual connection – an undeniable bond that creates a magnetic force. It's a feeling of certainty, a sense of belonging and a clarity of purpose that you've never felt before – and now you've tasted it, you never want to go back.

Remember that deliciously romantic scene from *Bridget Jones's Diary* when Mark Darcy (Colin Firth) tells Bridget (Renée Zellweger) that he likes her just the way she is? In the presence of your Twin Flame, there's no need to be anything other than who you are. You no longer need to earn their love or lose yourself in the process of receiving it. You are enough, just as you are. The love between you is unconditional and pure, and it holds the power to heal, transform and elevate your very being. You don't have to prove anything. You simply need to *be*.

This life-altering love – often referred to as Twin Flame love – is something that's been gaining more and more mainstream attention in recent years. Yet, as this chapter will make clear, its origins stretch back to ancient times, long before it became a buzzword. It's rooted in the timeless belief that each of us has a counterpart, a twin soul that shares your spiritual DNA or energy – a Spiritual Mirror that offers you a chance to truly see and know yourself beyond your human form. You could liken the concept to that of identical twins, who come from the same egg, split in two, and are separate but equal parts of the original whole.

Your Other Half

'Love is born into every human being; it calls back the halves of our original nature together; it tries to make one out of two and heal the wound of human nature. Each of us, then, is a "matching half" of a human whole – and each of us is always seeking the half that matches.'

—Plato

For the Ancient Greek philosopher Plato, the concept of Twin Flames was key. He believed that Twin Flames were two halves of the one soul, destined to reunite. In human form, they are drawn together by an innate longing to find each other and become a whole soul again. This idea of finding your 'other half', or someone who feels too compatible to be true, has been expressed in countless stories throughout history; the chances are, it resonates deeply within you. There is something indescribably alluring about the idea of meeting someone who makes you feel seen, heard, loved and validated in the purest way – someone who feels like your missing piece or other half.

The moment you meet your Spiritual Mirror – whether it strikes you suddenly, like a thunderbolt, or gradually builds over time – is a life-altering experience. It has the power to transform everything. The connection defies reason, logic and conventional understanding. It transcends everything you've been taught about love, relationships and the purpose of your life.

If you've ever questioned whether Twin Flame love is real or simply a romantic fantasy, I invite you to consider this: perhaps you haven't yet met your Twin Flame. Or, perhaps, you have yet to fully understand the true purpose of Cosmic Love, which in essence is the evolution of your soul. It is not just about feeling loved; it is about *becoming* love itself.

The journey to experiencing the richest, most transformative love is not passive. It requires you to transcend everything you've been conditioned to believe about love, relationships and yourself. It's about breaking free from the limitations of your past and allowing the unconditional, healing love of the Twin Flame to awaken your fullest potential. This is the one true journey of spiritual growth, a journey of becoming whole again.

Twin Flame Path Exercise:
Conjuring Your Twin Flame

Pause a little now and take a moment to reflect on what the term Twin Flame truly means to you. I encourage you to leap deeper into your own understanding and feel into the essence of what it might be like to meet the one who mirrors and completes your soul. To move your desires from dreams to reality.

Find a quiet space where you can reflect in peace. Grab a blank sheet of paper or open a digital document. Close your eyes for a moment, take a deep breath and ask yourself: What does the term 'Twin Flame' ignite within you? What emotions arise when you think about it? Do you believe that your Spiritual Mirror exists? And if so, where do you imagine they are?

Next, I'd like you to go a step further. Visualize, describe in words or imagine what your Twin Flame, your other half or the missing part of your soul might look like. What do they wear? What is their voice like? What qualities do they have? Picture their lifestyle, their values, their energy, with clarity. Bring them alive behind your eyes. No more vagueness. Be specific. Go into as much detail as feels right. If your Twin Flame were a character in a book, a movie, or a TV show, how would you draw or describe them?

This exercise is about connecting with the energy of your Twin Flame – whether or not you've already met them. The details don't matter as much as the feelings and the sense of connection and feelings of completeness the exercise inspires. Let yourself have fun with this. Let your imagination flow, without judgment or constraint.

Take a few minutes to jot down a few key words or a few sentences to capture the essence of this vision. Don't worry about writing a long essay – what's most important is the *quality* of your reflection, not its volume. This is an exercise in feeling and knowing, not perfection.

Once you've written your thoughts, save them in a place that's private to you. You can revisit this love note to yourself as you move through the chapters of this book, and it can become a powerful motivational tool to reflect on your evolving journey towards love.

This is the beginning of a deeper exploration – an opening of your heart to the possibility of your Divine Union changing from myth to reality, and to the transformative power of love that is meant to heal, empower and guide you towards your highest self, your higher love.

A Tale As Old As Time

The concept of Twin Flames speaks to a powerful universal longing within every soul: the desire to love deeply and fully, and to be loved in return with equal intensity. This longing isn't a passing desire – it's a sacred need embedded within your very nature. Exploring the origin and history of Twin Flames not only enriches your understanding of higher love but also empowers you to transcend the misconceptions that often cloud the concept in today's world.

My hope is that, by the end of this chapter, you'll be free from any misleading myths that have held you captive and that you'll reclaim the purity of your own understanding. This is crucial because, as the Law of Attraction states, *like energy attracts like energy*. If the energy of your beliefs about love is shaped by superficial or external sources, rather than your own inner wisdom, you'll unknowingly block the very connection you're seeking with your Twin Flame.

In today's world, social media floods our consciousness with the term 'Twin Flame', leading many to think that it's a New (or Now) Age concept. But in truth, the idea of Divine Union is as old as time. As mentioned above, perhaps the earliest reference to this connection can be found in the writings of the Ancient Greek philosopher Plato. While Plato didn't use the term Twin Flame (which is a contemporary construct), his dialogue *The Symposium* presents the theory of the 'split soul', which is remarkably similar.

According to Plato, humans were once hermaphrodite light beings – powerful entities with two faces, four arms and four legs. These beings were created to serve the gods, but their strength became so overwhelming that the gods feared a rebellion. To weaken them, the gods split them into two halves – one face, one set of limbs and one set of genitals. This division robbed them of their potency and, as a result, they became less inclined to live with purpose.

Apollo, the son of Zeus, saw the plight of these split souls and devised a plan to help them. He proposed that humans could be reunited with their other halves, but only if they were driven by a shared sense of purpose and desire. The gods ensured that these divided souls were scattered far and wide, so finding each other was a challenge. Each person would carry a belly button – a reminder that their Twin Flame existed somewhere, calling them to search for this missing piece of themselves. If these souls ever found each other, their power would be godlike; but they would also be so consumed with the joy of finding each other that they would want for nothing else.

When Twin Flames meet, Plato suggests, they are struck by the classic 'love at first sight' thunderbolt of desire and belonging – a powerful sensation of feeling complete. The souls become 'lost in an amazement of love and friendship and intimacy', forever drawn to each other, never wanting to part. Aristotle, a contemporary of Plato, echoed this sentiment, stating, 'Love is composed of a single soul inhabiting two bodies.'

The metaphors of the Twin Flame connection don't stop in Plato's works. The Ancient Greeks frequently referenced it in their mythology too – for instance, in the passionate yet forbidden love between Aphrodite, the goddess of love, and Ares, the god of war. Despite their stark differences and Aphrodite's inconvenient marriage to the unattractive god Hephaestus, the pull between her and Ares was undeniable. Their love, though fraught with divine punishment and separation, could never be broken. Their union produced children, including Eros (Cupid), the god of desire – suggesting that Divine Unions can create divine sparks.

In Hindu mythology, the sacred union between Shiva (the god of eternal love) and his consort Shakti embodies the same balance of masculine and feminine energies, mirroring the essence of the Twin Flame relationship. Within Christianity, there are references to the idea of the mirror soul, such as the creation of Eve from Adam's rib in the Old Testament: Book of

Genesis. And the theme of soul unity runs through the fabric of modern Western collective spirituality, reminding us of a greater cosmic connection between the feminine and masculine principles.

In Eastern philosophies like Buddhism, the complementary forces of Yin and Yang also represent this duality. Yin and Yang are opposing energies – feminine and masculine – that, when balanced, create harmony. The tension between these forces generates a dynamic energy that fuels success, growth and unity. On both personal and collective levels, the path to spiritual and emotional equilibrium comes through finding the balance of these energies within oneself.

The archetype of the Twin Flame is woven throughout the annals of global history, religion, mythology and philosophy. Whether in art, literature, cultural or religious texts, the return to the theme of higher love can always be found.

Twin Flames Present

Shakespeare's immortal play *Romeo and Juliet* spoke to the overwhelming force of Divine Union, where love is so intense that it transcends the boundaries of reason and circumstance. But, as outlined above, long before Shakespeare's tragic lovers, the concept of the Twin Flame had been explored by thought leaders, and it continues to be explored by visionaries to this day.

Interest in Twin Flames – the ancient idea of a soul split into two, destined to reunite in an eternal, unbreakable bond – has positively surged in recent decades. While the notion already existed in various spiritual traditions, the term as it is used today was first popularized for a mainstream audience in the late 1970s and early 1980s by Elizabeth Clare, an American spiritual teacher and founder of the Church Universal. Clare's teachings on this subject have had a lasting influence – and if you are intrigued you can still find her original lectures and insights online, offering a deeper exploration into the Twin Flame experience.

As an aside, an interesting personal synchronicity occurred during my research for this book, which felt like a gentle affirmation that I was meant to write it. Elizabeth Clare and I share the same birthday – 8 April. Coincidentally, this date is also the birthday of the Buddha in Japan. There is another layer of meaning too: as I note in one of the most popular books I've written, *The Element Encyclopedia of Birthdays*, 8 April is also the birthday of people characterized by Noble Intention – a fitting theme for the Twin Flame Journey.

Around the same time as Elizabeth Clare was teaching on Twin Flames, the idea was expanded upon by another influential figure, Dolores Cannon, an American author and hypnotherapist. She introduced the concept of two souls reincarnating together, meeting time and time again across lifetimes until they finally united. If you're drawn to the idea of reincarnation, I highly encourage you to explore Dolores Cannon's original teachings, which are also available online.

Since then, the term Twin Flame has woven itself into modern spiritual discourse, especially in the New Age community. The idea has also gained traction in mainstream celebrity culture and TV, often associated with romantic love.

However, its increased popularity has brought with it several misunderstandings and misconceptions.

Many people, having been swept up by the romantic allure of the idea, believe they have found their Twin Flame, only to later discover that they are instead involved in a Soul Mate, Karmic, or False Flame relationship. As the next chapter will make clear, it is crucial to recognize the differences between these dynamics, as the Twin Flame Journey is not simply about finding a romantic or lifetime partner.

The popular narrative that Spiritual Mirrors are destined to be with one another effortlessly, as if by magic, transcending time and space, is incredibly misleading. The truth is far more complex. The Twin Flame Voyage is one of profound spiritual healing and transformation. It is not without its challenges; it is sometimes deeply painful and tumultuous. It is not about seeking the perfect romantic partner or living in constant bliss. In fact, it can feel like a journey through darkness at times, but it is precisely in that darkness that the seeds of a higher, more unconditional love are planted.

If you feel like something is missing in your life or your relationships, and if you are willing to open your mind, surrender your preconceptions and consider the possibility that your understanding of love might need to evolve, then you are ready to begin your journey to a higher form of love in earnest. Beginning your Twin Flame Journey does not require you to be in a relationship or even to be seeking one. It requires only that you are ready to embark on the path of self-discovery and spiritual awakening. It is about returning to the love that is already within you, regardless of your relationship status.

As you begin this journey, you are likely to encounter many myths that need to be dumped. These misunderstandings can easily become roadblocks that delay your progress, so you will find them detailed and discharged for you systematically in the following section. Divine Union is not simply about finding someone to spend the rest of your life with, nor is it about the fairytale of love without effort. It is about reconnecting to the infinite love that exists within your own heart – from that connection, everything else will fall into place.

Dissecting Common Myths About Twin Flames

Before we head directly into the beating heart of your Twin Flame Awakening, it's important to clear away the common myths and misconceptions that can cloud your path. These illusions can keep you stuck, uncertain, or even sceptical about the existence of your Twin Flame. By letting go of these misunderstandings at the outset, you'll begin to awaken deeper truths within your heart – truths that may have long been forgotten but are always waiting for you to recall them.

A word of caution: The ingrained ideas below may take a while for your mind and heart to release, so take a moment to breathe deeply and ground yourself as often as you need. When you're ready to open yourself fully to a new perspective on love, let's begin.

Myth 1: 'You Need to Deserve Them First'

There's a grain of truth in this myth, but it's far from the whole story. While it's true that you need to cultivate inner peace and self-love before attracting a healthy Divine Union, the notion that you need to 'deserve' your Twin Flame is a trap.

Feeling like you aren't 'good enough' or that you need to become 'better' to deserve true love only keeps you in a loop of self-judgment and inadequacy. This self-doubt is a form of self-harm, holding you back from seeing the beauty of who you are right now, imperfections and all.

You are not incomplete. You are whole and your flaws are not your weakness; they are your pathways to growth, healing and self-discovery. The Twin Flame Journey isn't about striving for an impossible perfection in yourself and another person. It's about embracing who you are and having compassion for your journey, including the mistakes you make along the way. Just as you learn to love and accept yourself through your imperfections, you'll learn to do the same for others – especially your Spiritual Mirror. Love isn't about fixing yourself to fit someone else's ideal; it's about learning from your flaws, loving everything about yourself and from there evolving into your highest self with grace.

Myth 2: 'They Are Your Other Half'

This idea, popularized by Plato's notion of split souls, is more poetic than practical. As Myth 1 made clear, the truth is that you are already whole. Your soul isn't missing a part of itself wandering out there in the world.

Believing that your Twin Flame is your 'other half' creates a sense of dependence – like you need someone else to complete you or fill a void. This belief leads to the trap of waiting for someone to 'rescue' you from your loneliness or inner turmoil.

Meeting your Spiritual Mirror may activate a yearning for wholeness within you, but that doesn't mean you need them in your life to become whole. The Twin Flame Odyssey is about realizing that you already possess everything you need within yourself, with or without them. When you acknowledge this truth, you free yourself to live fully and authentically, knowing that you are enough – exactly as you are.

Myth 3: 'Your Twin Flame Is the Only Person Who Can Unbreak Your Heart'

When you meet your Twin Flame for the first time, it may feel like the most euphoric connection you've ever experienced. The intensity, the depth, the instant recognition – it is the most profound love you've ever known. You may understandably believe that this person is the source of all your happiness and healing; and in a sense, that's true. But here's where the myth comes in: your Twin Flame isn't the *source* of the love you feel – they are the *mirror* that reflects the love that already exists within you and which you are now tapping into.

The key to understanding your Twin Flame Journey is to recognize that the love you experience isn't external; it's simply the love within you being recognized and activated. Your Spiritual Mirror can spark a desire to rediscover that love, but they are not the source of it. You are. This is an empowering realization, as it places the power of healing and love squarely within your own hands. True love comes from within; and once you recognize that, you are free to explore your connection to others without dependency or expectation.

Myth 4: 'Finding Your Twin Flame Gives Your Life Its Purpose'

A prevalent myth is that finding your Twin Flame will finally give your life the meaning and purpose you've been seeking. But this is a dangerous illusion. Your purpose in life is not dependent on another person. Like love, your purpose is something that already resides within you, waiting to be discovered.

You don't need to wait until you find your perfect partner to live a life of purpose. Whether you're single or in a relationship, your purpose is yours to define. Your Spiritual Mirror can guide you towards recognizing your higher purpose, but the primary goal of the Twin Flame Journey is not to find a partner – it's to find yourself, to awaken the deep well of unconditional love, purpose, meaning and creativity already within you.

Myth 5: 'Twin Flames Are Connected by Invisible Strings'

While the idea of invisible strings connecting souls is a lovely metaphor, it doesn't entirely explain the nature of the Twin Flame relationship. The concept of invisible threads that bind people, places and situations together dates back centuries, found in traditions like the East Asian red thread of fate and the Western idea of destiny. It's also gaining popularity today, fuelled by songs like Taylor Swift's 'Invisible String'.

However, while this concept may complement your Twin Flame Evolution, it is not synonymous with it as it focuses on all aspects of life, not just the romantic. Divine Union also isn't about navigating an inescapable fate or destiny or believing in a higher power that's guiding you – it's about becoming aware of an energetic pull within you towards a higher love and then trusting the universe to guide you in the direction of a validating relationship.

Myth 6: 'Soul Mates and Twin Flames Are the Same Thing'

While Soul Mates and Twin Flames are often used interchangeably, they are distinct. Soul Mates come into your life to support your personal growth, offering harmony, love, or complementary energies. You can have several Soul Mates in your lifetime, each fulfilling a specific purpose, but you will have only one Twin Flame.

Your Twin Flame is the mirror of your heart and soul. The connection is unique, intense, challenging and transformative. Divine Unions aren't always easy, because someone who 'sees' you so completely can be alarming if you haven't done the inner work; but wherever you are with your personal growth, they serve as a powerful catalyst for self-awareness and spiritual growth.

Like any Soul Mate relationships that help expand your consciousness along the way, the Twin Flame bond is often a romantic one because the connection is so intimate. However, it is important to stress that the Twin Flame relationship and some Soul Mate partnerships are not always romantic – they are primarily about your soul's evolution.

Myth 7: 'Once You Find Your Twin Flame, You Must Never Separate'

Many people believe that once you meet your Twin Flame, you are destined to be together forever. But unconditional love does not bind you to another person. It inspires you to become the best that you can be and then sets you free.

The idea that you must stay with your Twin Flame, no matter the circumstances, can create unhealthy dependency. Spiritual Mirrors can exist in many forms, sometimes apart, sometimes together. Separation can happen – either physically or emotionally – but it doesn't invalidate the energetic or unseen bond you share.

Twin Flame love is unconditional; and even when you are apart, the energy of the love between you continues to transform you, propelling you towards your higher purpose.

Myth 8: 'You Need to Search for Your Twin Flame Until You Find Them'

Chasing after Cosmic Love is counterproductive. Higher love is something you attract, not chase. The more you focus on understanding and healing yourself, cultivating self-love and aligning with your inner truth, the more you will draw your Twin Flame to you – without effort.

Your Spiritual Mirror is always connected to you on an energetic level, whether you're actively searching for them or not. This book serves as your compass to help you navigate your Twin Flame Journey and listen to the guiding wisdom of your own heart.

Myth 9: 'Twin Flame Relationships Are Always Romantic'

As mentioned above, although Divine Unions are often romantic, they don't have to be. Your Spiritual Mirror might be a platonic friend, a family member, a mentor, or anyone with whom you share a profound, life-changing connection. The journey isn't always about romance or physical love; it's about spiritual awakening, a higher love.

Myth 10: 'Seeing 11:11 Means Your Twin Flame Is Near'

Seeing repeating numbers like 11:11 is often associated with Twin Flame synchronicities, but it's not a definitive sign that your Twin Flame is physically near. It is more likely a reminder from the universe that the energetic connection exists and that your yearning for inner wholeness is real and something worth believing in and fighting for.

Myth 11: 'Your Twin Flame Searches for You Across Space and Time'

Only if you believe in the possibility of time travel, the existence of an afterlife and reincarnation. The famous 1980 romantic fantasy movie *Somewhere in Time* tells the love story of a 1970s screenwriter called Richard (played by Christopher Reeves) who manifests himself back to 1912 so he can meet Elise (played by Jane Seymour) after becoming obsessed with a photograph of her. The two fall instantly in love but Richard dies of a broken heart when he is unwillingly transported back to 1980.

However, their love goes on as the pair are reunited forever once they reach the afterlife.

The power of Cosmic Love surviving death also features in the epic love story of Jack (Leonardo DiCaprio) and Rose (Kate Winslet) in the haunting closing scene of the 1998 movie *Titanic*, which I defy anyone to watch without shedding a tear, and in *What Dreams May Come*, another iconic film from 1998, starring the late, great Robin Williams.

Although there is tentative research suggesting the possibility of consciousness surviving bodily death in a near-death experience, and mediums allegedly communicate with the world of spirit, for now the question of whether an afterlife exists remains a matter of belief. There is no proof. However, if you believe that everything in this universe is energy, including your consciousness – and that energy cannot be destroyed, only transformed – it is conceivable that your consciousness may be able to survive bodily death. And if survival is possible, the idea that your consciousness or soul can choose to reincarnate or be born again in another human body seems plausible too.

Twin Flames are said to reincarnate together as a way of raising the energetic vibration of Earth to bring humanity closer to love and unity. What your heart chooses to believe is entirely personal, and this book will not attempt to influence your choice of belief in any way. All I will say is that, enticing as the idea of afterlife and reincarnation sounds, it can sometimes distract us from the power of now.

While the idea of love transcending time is deeply romantic, it's not the reality of living and loving your Twin Flame Path.

The most important thing on your Twin Flame Journey is to stay grounded in the present moment.

Myth 12: 'Your Twin Flame Is Your Divine Masculine/Feminine'

Your Twin Flame is not simply an opposite- or same-sex counterpart. Your soul contains both masculine and feminine energies, as does the soul of your Twin Flame. The journey isn't about finding someone who completes you based on gender – it's about finding someone who mirrors your soul's divine energy, regardless of gender.

Myth 13: 'Only I Can Help You Find Your Twin Flame'

While many teachers claim to have the secret knowledge to help you find your Divine Union – and there are stacks of costly coaches and courses out there – please be wary. The only compass you need is your own heart. Trust your own intuition, because it will never lead you astray. If anyone tells you they can 'find' your Twin Flame for you, and 'know' who is right for you, they are leading you in the wrong direction.

Your Love Guru

By dispelling these myths, you clear the fog around your Twin Flame Adventure. The more you let go of these misconceptions, the more clarity you will gain, allowing your heart to lead you towards true spiritual growth and unconditional love. Indeed, as you embark on your Twin Flame Journey, one of the most powerful truths you'll immediately encounter is that you don't need to search far and wide or look to experts for the guidance you seek. You already have a remarkable mentor waiting to lead you. This guide has been with you since the moment you drew your first breath, quietly loving you, supporting you, protecting you, and always waiting for the moment when you would finally recognize and treasure it. That guide is your heart – your truest mentor, your most loyal companion, beating with anticipation, ready to help you discover its true love wisdom.

Your life on Earth begins with the first beat of your heart and ends when your heart stops beating. But your heart is not just a physical organ – it is the centre of your emotional and intuitive life. In many ancient traditions, the heart is seen as the true seat of awareness and power, a direct link to the divine. It is the sacred place where your body, mind and soul unite, a place that holds the secrets to everlasting love. If you desire to attract the love you seek, the journey begins here – within the depths of your own heart.

To truly connect with your heart's wisdom, you must consciously shift your focus inwards. The world of dating and romance constantly calls your attention outwards, but the miracle of love, true love, is not found in external pursuits. It is found in the stillness and joy of your own being. Your heart is the first place to look for the higher love you've been longing for, and it is the only place that will lead you to the Cosmic Love you desire. The beating of your heart is a love guru, constantly offering you direction – if you know how to listen.

Every moment, including this one, your heart is quietly steering you towards what and who will complete you. The challenge, in the rush of daily life, is that we often fail to hear its whispers. It can be easy to overlook the subtle nudges your heart sends, to dismiss its guidance in favour of the louder, more chaotic and obvious distraction and noise of the outside world. But if you take the time to focus, you will begin to hear your heart's wisdom talking to you with clarity. It knows, often long before you do, what is right for you – who is meant for you, what next steps to take and when the timing is right.

Tell It to Your Heart

Modern research now supports the ancient wisdom that the heart possesses a unique power that extends beyond its biological function. Studies by the HeartMath Institute reveal that when you experience emotions like love, joy, creativity and peace, your heart enters a state of harmony – what they call 'heart coherence'.[3] In this state, your heart beats in a calm, steady rhythm that aligns with your body and mind, creating an optimal state of being. This coherence is not just a metaphor; it's a tangible, measurable physiological state that promotes balance and clarity. In fact, when you are in this state, you are better equipped to make wise decisions, concentrate effectively and even improve your physical health.

On the flip side, when you experience emotions such as anger, fear, or stress, your heart rate becomes erratic and your body falls into a state of dissonance. The negative effects of stress on your heart health are well-documented and can hinder your ability to stay present and focused. When your heart is in dissonance, you may feel disconnected from your intuition, and this can cloud your judgment – making it harder to follow your Twin Flame Path.

When you can connect with your heart's energy, embracing feelings of love, peace and joy, you are operating at your highest vibrational frequency. In this state, you are physically, mentally and spiritually at your peak – and it is from this place of coherence that your Divine Union will naturally unfold.

To align more fully with your heart's wisdom, make a daily practice of tuning into it. Begin by simply listening to the rhythm of your heart, feeling its presence within you. The more you make this a conscious practice, the more natural it will become. Your intuitive abilities will grow not just in matters of love, but in all areas of your life. You will begin to trust your inner wisdom more deeply, knowing that your heart is a faithful guide on the path towards true love – and ultimately, the union of your soul with your Twin Flame.

Your heart already knows where and who your Twin Flame is. What you may need are the right tools – insights, practices and techniques – to align yourself with your heart's wisdom and draw your Spiritual Mirror closer. The good news is that researchers from the HeartMath Institute have identified key actions that keep the heart in a state of 'coherence' – a state of alignment and harmony that can guide you towards more fulfilling relationships and a more authentic life.

Below you will find a series of simple, yet profound rituals designed to achieve a state of heart coherence. These rituals are to be practised daily or as often as you can, allowing you to continually reinforce the importance of connecting with your heart's wisdom.

Remember, the journey to your deepest connection begins not by searching outside of yourself but by going inwards to the sacred space within where love has found its happily ever after home – your heart.

Reconnect With Your Heart

This simple exercise will help you reconnect with the unseen, intuitive power of your heart. It's a practice that can be done anywhere, at any time, and it will help you to create a more powerful relationship with the most authentic part of yourself.

Place your hand on your heart. Take a moment to gently place the fingers and palm of your left hand on the centre of your chest, over your heart. Allow the touch to be soft and tender, as if you are offering compassion to yourself. Feel the warmth of your hand as it connects with your heart space. Let your touch be a reminder that you are honouring and nurturing this connection. Out loud or with your thoughts, tell your heart to 'wake up'.

Deepen your breath. Now, close your eyes (if it feels safe and appropriate to do so) and begin to breathe deeply. Take a slow, full inhale from your stomach, letting your breath rise upwards through your nose. Hold it for a moment, then exhale gently through your mouth, releasing all the air from your lungs. Do this for several breaths, allowing each one to become slower and deeper. With each inhale, imagine you are drawing in peace, love and wisdom. With each exhale, imagine you are letting go of any tension or distractions.

Tune in to the rhythm of your heart. As you continue breathing, bring your attention to the sound and sensation of your heartbeat. Is it fast or steady? Is it in sync, or does it feel irregular? Listen carefully, not just with your ears but with your emotions. Feel the rhythm, the pulse, the life force that flows within you. If you have trouble sensing it, simply remain still and patient for a while longer – your heart will speak to you in time.

If you prefer to keep your eyes open, just focus on the sensation of your heart beating, feeling the pulse within your chest. Tune in to this natural rhythm. There is wisdom in every beat. Let it guide you back to yourself.

Focus on heart-focused breathing. When you feel grounded in the rhythm of your own heart, bring your focus to your breathing again, but now direct your attention specifically to your heart. With each inhale, imagine your breath flowing directly into your heart. With each exhale, imagine your breath flowing out from your heart, like a gentle wave.

Find a natural rhythm for your breath. A good starting point is to breathe in for 3–5 seconds and exhale for 3–5 seconds. Allow your breath to become a peaceful, steady cycle that mirrors the pulse of your heart. Feel the deep connection between your breath and your heart. This is your heart-centred breathing.

Make a daily heart reconnection. To truly strengthen your relationship with your heart, I encourage you to practise this exercise for a few minutes daily. Your heart holds the wisdom of your soul and is the greatest love guru you will ever have. It will guide you not only in matters of love but in every decision – how you think, feel, dream, speak and act.

Consider setting an alarm on your phone at the same time each day (mid-morning is ideal). When the alarm goes off, a simple word or heart emoji can appear on your screen as a reminder to pause and reconnect with the power of your heart. Allow this moment to remind you that your heart's wisdom is always available to you. In every decision, big or small, let your heart be included in the process. Remember, the more you tune in to your heart's wisdom, the more aligned you will become with your Twin Flame Path. Start today and make a promise to yourself to always trust and listen to your heart. It will never willingly lead you astray.

Your Brave-Heart Rituals

In the realm of the heart, thoughts and words hold little power unless they are grounded in action. This is why rituals are so effective. Rituals are not bound by any religious tradition. They are, at their core, intentional and meaningful actions that invite you to honour the present moment and the energy within you. Rituals are distinct from habits, which are actions performed automatically, often without mindfulness or gratitude. When you engage in a ritual, you are bringing presence and purpose to what you do, opening yourself to higher levels of spiritual awareness.

If you seek to accelerate your personal and spiritual growth – if you wish to align with your highest potential and the divine love that flows along your Twin Flame Path – then it is essential to perform daily heart-centred rituals. These rituals are designed to connect you to the powerful force of love that is always present, guiding you towards your highest truth.

While each ritual is supported by evidence of its effectiveness for easing stress, it's important to remember that the heart, much like the vast depths of the ocean, holds mysteries that cannot always be fully explained. What is clear, however, is that your heart is shaped by the most powerful and transformative force in the universe: love.

Heart-Reaction Ritual: Listening to Your Heart's Voice

You've already been introduced in this chapter to the practice of heart-focused breathing, a tool that helps you connect more deeply with the voice of your heart. Now, it's time to take your new heartfelt connection a step further. This next ritual invites you to consciously tune into your heartbeat before making any decisions, whether they concern relationships or anything else.

Take a few quiet moments to check in with your heart. Feel the rhythm of your heartbeat and let it guide your actions. No matter what decision is before you, pause first to take your pulse.

To do this: turn one hand over so it is palm-up, then gently place two fingertips of your other hand in the groove of your wrist, a couple of inches down from the base of your thumb. You should feel the steady pulsation of your heartbeat. Now, ask yourself:

'Is the beat steady and calm, or is it fast and racing?'
'What is my heart telling me?'

Ignore the chatter of your thoughts for a moment and turn your attention inwards. What does the wisdom of your heart say? Does it say *yes*? Does it say *no*? Or perhaps it whispers that more time is needed to decide.

Your heart, with its infinite wisdom, already knows what is best for you. If you ignore its messages, if you remain too busy or distracted to truly listen, you risk stumbling along your Twin Flame Journey. But when you learn to authentically connect to your heart, and to always consult it first, the answers you seek will become clear and you will be guided towards a more aligned and harmonious life.

Sacred Heart

The next batch of heart rituals are designed to connect you to the ancient, mystical power of shapes – symbols that hold deep spiritual significance and resonate on a level your heart understands best. These symbols carry within them energies that can shift your awareness, clear blockages and open you to divine guidance.

You are invited to work with these shapes in a way that feels right for you. You can draw or colour them, an act of concentration and flow that brings a sense of stillness and focus, like the state of meditation. Alternatively, you might choose to simply gaze at them or trace their outlines with your fingers. No matter how you choose to engage with these sacred shapes, do so with mindfulness and reverence, allowing the wisdom of your heart to speak through them.

As you engage in each ritual, observe the feelings and insights that arise within you. What messages does your heart wish to share with you? What direction is it offering you on your Twin Flame Path? Trust that your heart knows the best way for you, and let these symbols be a doorway through which you connect with your deeper wisdom.

These rituals are not meant to be understood only through the intellect; they are to be felt in the heart. Allow yourself to be guided by your inner knowing or intuition and let the power of these sacred practices lead you towards greater clarity and love.

Heart-Shifter Ritual: The Yin-Yang Symbol

The yin-yang symbol represents the presence of opposites within everything: light and dark, masculine and feminine, logic and intuition. This Ancient Chinese symbol teaches us that harmony and balance come from integrating these opposing forces within ourselves. We all carry both yin (the feminine, mystery, receptivity) and yang (the masculine, logic, action) energies within our hearts. True peace is found when these energies flow together seamlessly, creating balance within us.

> Spend a few moments studying the yin-yang symbol on the following page. Trace around it with your fingers, following the lines if you want to.
>
> Reflect on how this symbol speaks to you.
>
> If you feel drawn to, colour it in – either in this book or on a printout. Let the colours represent how you feel about

the balance between the masculine and feminine energies within you and the balance between logical and imaginative energies within you.

Ask yourself:

'What does my heart want this symbol to know about me?'

Journal your thoughts, paying attention to any inner messages that arise.

Heart-Shifter Ritual: The Labyrinth

A labyrinth is different from a maze. Unlike a maze, a labyrinth contains no dead ends, no wrong turns. The path twists and turns but always leads to the centre. In many ancient cultures, walking a labyrinth was a spiritual practice, a ritual for deep reflection and connection. In these rituals, the labyrinth represents life's journey – sometimes we feel lost, but each turn is part of our evolution. The path to true love, especially the journey towards your Twin Flame, often mirrors this process. It may feel confusing or challenging in the moment, but every step is guiding you to your heart.

Focus on the labyrinth image below (or one that you have created on paper or with objects you have to hand).

Trace the path with your finger or gaze, imagining yourself walking through it.

As you journey to the centre of the labyrinth, visualize this path as the journey to the core of your heart. Trust the winding path of your life and that every challenge, twist and turn is leading you closer to the truth of your heart.

What insights or messages arise as you 'walk' this path?

Reflect on any obstacles or turns that have shaped your path to true love or self-love.

Note: If you want to physically walk a labyrinth, you can create one yourself using cardboard or with small objects in your home. Alternatively, you can refer to http://www.labyrinthlocator.com to see whether there is a labyrinth local to you.

Heart-Shifter Ritual: Mandala

The word 'mandala' comes from the ancient traditions of Buddhism and Hinduism and means simply 'circle'. The circle represents wholeness, unity and the infinite cycle of life. Mandalas are used as tools for meditation, self-reflection and spiritual connection. They encourage us to journey inwards, unlocking wisdom from within our own hearts. When you gaze at or create a mandala, you are connecting with your deepest, most authentic self.

Focus on the mandala design on the following page (or one that you have created).

Allow your gaze to soften and absorb the intricate details of the design.

As you do so, take deep, mindful breaths and invite your heart's wisdom to emerge.

Let your mind wander, but gently return to the mandala whenever you notice your focus drifting.

What messages does your heart reveal as you focus on this sacred symbol?

Heart-Shifter Ritual: Colour Your Heart

The act of colouring or filling in a heart symbol is a creative way to reflect on the unique energy of your heart in this present moment. Through this exercise, you will tap into the vibrant, ever-evolving energy of your emotions and self-love.

Draw a heart shape on a blank piece of paper or use the simple outline provided on the following page.

Colour in the heart, either using pens, pencils or paints or in your mind's eye.

Choose colours that represent how you feel in this moment – what is your heart expressing?

Reflect on why you chose these colours. Research the traditional meanings of the colours – but remember that what matters most is what they mean to you.

Allow your heart to come alive as you focus on the colours and feel their energy.

You don't have to stick to just one colour. You can use a mix of colours, creating a rainbow of feelings within your heart.

Be honest with yourself – this is not about making a 'pretty' heart. Life is messy, and so is the heart. You can create a beautiful image full of contradictions and complexities, just as your own heart contains both joy and sorrow, light and shadow. Celebrate every emotion and honour your heart's journey.

As this entry-level chapter draws to a close, one key truth has clearly emerged: the only way forward on your spiritual journey is by returning, time and again, to the wisdom of your heart – not someone else's heart, even if you feel they are your Twin Flame, but *yours*. When you lose touch with the uniqueness of your heart, you lose your direction in life.

Remember that the ritual exercises in this chapter are designed to help you unlock the wisdom and power of your heart. Your heart is not a static place; it is ever evolving. These rituals invite you to celebrate that fluidity and deepen your self-awareness, bringing you closer and closer to the love and truth within you.

Closer and Closer to Love

From the mystic teachings of ancient civilizations to the celebrity headlines of today, the concept of Cosmic Love continues to captivate us. It's an idea that stirs the soul, igniting hope and longing. But here's an important question: if your heart is the ultimate source of unconditional love and finding love within first is essential, do you *really* need a Twin Flame in your life?

The answer is both simple and profound, like your heart.

No – in the sense that you are already a complete soul, whole and capable of experiencing the bliss of divine love without the need for a Divine Union. You don't need another person to feel the fullness of love within you.

But also *yes, yes, yes!* – in the sense that the longing for your Twin Flame can serve as a powerful catalyst, an energetic driving force that pushes you towards deeper growth and gives your life meaning and purpose. The belief in the real possibility of meeting your Twin Flame in person at any moment can excite, energize and inspire you to evolve in ways you never imagined. It sparks an intense desire to evolve into your highest self. So, while you don't need a Twin Flame in your life to experience love, *your longing for them* can lead you towards the highest form of love you will ever know: the unconditional love for yourself and others that resides within your own heart.

Coming Attractions

I trust that the insights shared in this chapter have illuminated your understanding of Twin Flames, sparking a light that burns brighter than it did before you began this journey. Be gentle with yourself if you find that you still need time for some of these concepts to fully sink in. Spiritual wisdom doesn't always reveal itself in an instant, like a 'road to Damascus' epiphany, and that's okay. Feel free to revisit this chapter as many times as needed until it begins to make perfect sense.

If you choose to embark on the heart rituals discussed, please commit to them daily for at least four weeks – this is the minimum time researchers believe it takes to begin rewiring the brain[4] and shifting deeply ingrained mindsets towards healing. Patience is essential. Remember, the ideas about love that shape your current worldview didn't develop overnight. These beliefs were formed over a lifetime, from childhood onwards, and they require time and gentle effort to change.

You're not just learning about love; you're discovering a whole new way of experiencing and becoming it. So, take your time. Live and love the process as it unfolds.

It's also completely natural for confusion to arise on your Twin Flame Pilgrimage, particularly when it comes to distinguishing between Soul Mates and Twin Flames. This is a challenge your heart will encounter repeatedly on your path, and you're not alone in this. That's why, in the next chapter, we will plunge ever deeper into Soul Mate and other Karmic relationships. By the time we're done, you'll have a clear understanding of how these special relationships differ from the unique bond of a Spiritual Mirror.

And so, as you continue this journey, please be kind to yourself and stay curious, for the Twin Flame Path to higher love is only beginning to reveal its infinite wonders to you. Know that the beautiful revelations meant for you will come to pass in their own perfect time. A love greater than you've ever imagined awaits. Look. It is already beckoning to you on the horizon.

2

KARMIC BONDS, FALSE FLAMES AND SOUL MATES

Throughout your life, you will likely experience a variety of intimate relationships, each offering valuable lessons and challenges. These relationships can generally be categorized into four types: Karmic, False Flame, Soul Mate and Twin Flame.

While the next chapter will warmly explore Twin Flame relationships, this one will focus on Karmic, False Flame and Soul Mate relationships. Understanding and learning from these key relationships is crucial before you are ready for the full-on experience of Divine Union. They are not random; they play an essential role in your personal growth, teaching you crucial lessons about self-awareness and the nature of love.

No one simply wakes up to find their Twin Flame waiting for them. The journey to this deep, resonant connection requires preparation – growth, learning and inner healing. In essence, it is through navigating Karmic, False Flame and Soul Mate relationships that you prepare your heart and ready yourself for Divine Union.

Twin Flames are not inherently 'superior' relationships; they simply serve a higher purpose. However, there is a kind of progression: before your Twin Flame can fully enter your life, you must experience the heart-deep lessons offered by other kinds of relationships.

A Word About Integration

Achieving Divine Union is only possible when you stop projecting your unmet needs or repressed emotions onto others. You learn how to nurture and address them within yourself. Self-sufficiency – the ability to find what you typically seek from others within yourself – is a crucial part of your Twin Flame Journey because it acts like a magnet to your higher Cosmic Love. And the voyage of personal growth that leads to self-sufficiency is known as *integration*.

The concept of integration was introduced by the Swiss psychiatrist and founder of analytical psychology Carl Jung (1875–1961). He posited that the psyche, or personality, is made up of many different parts, including the inner child, the persona, the anima and animus, the shadow and the Self. All these different parts need to be acknowledged, understood and integrated.

In this chapter, you'll encounter references to these different aspects of your personality because your path to personal growth and wholeness – which must unfold before Divine Union can happen – requires you to consciously become aware of and integrate them all, most especially the anima and animus.

Jung's groundbreaking theory of the *collective unconscious* suggests that every individual carries both masculine and feminine energies within themselves – represented by the archetypes of the anima (feminine aspect) and the animus (masculine aspect). According to Jung, the anima is the feminine part of the male psyche, and the animus is the masculine part of the female psyche. These internal aspects shape our perceptions of gender and relationships, and their integration is crucial for personal growth and loving relationships.

When the anima and animus are in balance, they provide the foundation for healthy relationships and psychological wellbeing. An integrated anima brings qualities like empathy, creativity and emotional nurturing, while an integrated animus offers assertiveness, rationality and the ability to take action and manifest ideas. The integration of these twin energies within oneself is a powerful catalyst for personal and spiritual growth that can create a magnetic inner Twin Flame dynamic.

In essence, to truly encounter your Spiritual Mirror, you must first learn to balance and harmonize – or, in Jungian terminology, integrate – unexpressed or conflicting energies within, or become whole from the inside out. Only then can you attract the one who mirrors you – your other half, in the fullest, most rewarding sense.

Shades of Love

At times, certain relationships will naturally fade from your life once they've fulfilled their purpose. You have learned the personal-growth lessons they were meant to teach you, and you may feel ready to release them and step into a higher level of emotional and spiritual growth. However, this letting go of significant relationships in your life isn't always smooth sailing. It can be deeply traumatic.

After the pain of letting go of a particularly intense connection, you might find yourself feeling drained or completely disillusioned with the idea of love. The urge to protect your heart can become overwhelming, and the thought of opening yourself up to love again may feel frightening. You may feel deeply sceptical about the possibility of meeting your 'forever person'.

I hope this chapter can serve as a potent antidote to that cynicism. It's important to remember that intimate relationships – whether they bring you pain or joy, whether they last for a season or a lifetime – are a beautiful and invaluable part of your personal and spiritual evolution. Relationships are not bound by any rigid expectations or timelines. They exist to help you transcend the limitations of what you've been taught love is, so that you can discover your own unique understanding of it. And, as you come to understand what love truly means to you, you also uncover who you are at your core.

The more you experience, learn and grow, the more aligned you are with your truest self; and the more aligned you are with your authentic self, the more likely you are to attract your Twin Flame. Every relationship, even the most painful ones, brings wisdom that shapes you and prepares you for deeper love and connection, so never regret time spent loving someone else. Love is not just about finding your perfect partner; it's about discovering and evolving into the loving and fulfilled person you are meant to be.

So, before we delve into the stages and signs of Twin Flame relationships in the next chapter, let's reflect here on the other three significant relationship categories that shape your heart and help prepare you for Cosmic Love. Though they may share strong similarities with the Twin Flame, their purpose is distinct. Understanding the differences between them is essential on your path to self-discovery and higher love.

Let's begin with those breathtaking but ever so tricky to navigate Karmic bonds.

What Is a Karmic Relationship?

If you have been in one of those relationships when it is sunshine and roses one minute and then fierce arguments the next, or a cycle of make-up and break-up, each phase more harrowing than the next so you never know where you stand, the chances are you have been deep in a Karmic entanglement.

This is typically love that feels fast and furious, intense, unresolved and confusing. You may often feel that you are so close to a perfect relationship but then you let yourself down or your partner lets you down or you both let each other down. You may spend hours talking things through with them in the hope of finding the magic solution, or you may bite your tongue and behave in ways that are not authentic to you for the sake of saving your relationship. Time and time again, your good intentions fail.

A great deal of your energy is spent worrying about the relationship and what you or they said, felt or did. You may seek relationship advice from family, friends or counsellors, desperately hoping they will give you that one piece of advice that makes everything right. A part of you could get hooked on the drama, so you start to believe that this is the nature of passion.

And if one Karmic relationship ends and you haven't learned the lesson it was meant to teach you, then the chances are extremely high that you will jump right into another one, hoping that the ending will be somehow different this time. It won't. I learned this the hard way.

My first serious relationship happened in my early twenties, and, like many Karmic bonds, it was a tempestuous and life-altering experience. There was instant, undeniable chemistry, the kind that feels fated. It was love at first sight, but with that intensity came insecurity, jealousy and emotional chaos – a rollercoaster of break-ups, reunions and tears. I lost myself in that relationship. I defined myself by it. When it ended, I felt a grief so deep, so all-consuming, it was as if I had lost a part of myself.

That wasn't the last Karmic romantic connection, though. The cycle continued until I learned to break free from my co-dependent, people-pleasing patterns and nurture my inner child. It was rinse and repeat. But I grew a little wiser each time. I began to see what these relationships were meant to teach me about self-love, boundaries and healing.

If you are wondering whether you are in a Karmic relationship right now, you need to ask yourself whether trying to make the relationship work, and fear of what others think about the relationship, are more important than whether this relationship is indeed right for you. How much of yourself have you invested in the relationship? If you aren't sure, the answer is 'too much' and you are likely tangled up in a restrictive Karmic bond.

Karmic relationships are often confused with Twin Flames because the love you feel for the other person is instant and intense. But you need to understand that the reason you fell in love with your Karmic partner at first sight is that they speak directly to your neglected inner child. And it is that inner child, not the relationship itself, that is screaming for your undivided love and attention.

Healing the Inner Child in Karmic Relationships

Karmic relationships are connections that tend to be deeply rooted in unresolved issues, typically from childhood experiences or, if you believe in reincarnation, past lives. These relationships manifest your inner struggles, unhealed pain and emotional imbalances. The concept of karma suggests that actions from previous lifetimes – or earlier in this one – create energetic imprints that influence your current experiences. In Karmic relationships, these imprints are triggered, requiring deep inner healing for personal and spiritual growth to unfold.

At the heart of a Karmic relationship is the need to nurture the inner child – a sometimes hidden part of you that holds the purity, innocence, passion and creativity you experienced as a child as well as unresolved wounds, unmet needs and hefty emotional baggage. Often, when two people enter a Karmic relationship, they unconsciously seek to heal these past traumas through their interactions. This can lead to a dynamic that feels intense and often triggering on every level.

The energy exchange can be imbalanced, with one or both individuals re-enacting familiar patterns of co-dependency, emotional manipulation, or unresolved anger from their early years. These relationships can become addictive, as each person may feel drawn to the other to resolve those childhood wounds or past hurts. While the love in these relationships may feel powerful, it is rooted in unhealed needs for validation, parenting and emotional regulation, rather than genuine connection.

The primary lesson of a Karmic relationship is to recognize these patterns and focus on healing your inner child. It's about taking responsibility for your own healing and learning to love yourself without depending on another person to 'fix', 'parent', nurture, support or complete you. Until you can do this – until you can understand and nurture your own inner child – your heart will just not be ready to meet your Twin Flame.

Case Study: A Karmic Relationship and the Path to Healing

Sarah and David's story offers a powerful example of a Karmic relationship shining the spotlight on unmet needs. Their connection began with fiery passion but quickly spiralled into pain and confusion, leaving them both with lasting lessons about self-worth, healing and growth.

Sarah grew up in an environment where emotional neglect and criticism were constant companions. Her parents, though loving in their own way, never seemed able to provide the emotional validation and acceptance she so desperately needed. As a result, Sarah developed a sense of inadequacy that followed her into adulthood.

She carried an unspoken fear of not being enough and this often manifested as a desperate need for approval in her relationships. She was a people-pleaser.

David, on the other hand, had faced his own emotional turmoil. After a painful break-up in his early twenties, he carried the scars of rejection and abandonment. This experience left him with a deep-seated fear that anyone he got close to would eventually leave him. He became emotionally guarded, creating walls around his heart to protect himself from further pain.

When Sarah and David met, they seemed to fit together like two pieces of a puzzle – each feeling the other could offer the emotional security they craved. Sarah was drawn to David's seeming confidence, while David was captivated by Sarah's warmth. However, their bond quickly revealed itself to be more than just romantic attraction; it was a Karmic tie, one that would push both to confront their unresolved emotional wounds.

In the beginning, their connection was all-consuming. They shared an intense closeness and it felt like their relationship had been predestined. But as time wore on, their individual insecurities began to surface. Sarah's unresolved feelings of inadequacy would often turn into jealousy and controlling behaviour, as she sought reassurance from David. In turn, David's fear of being abandoned triggered emotional withdrawal on his part. When things became too intense, he would retreat, leaving Sarah feeling alone and misunderstood.

This cyclical pattern created constant emotional storms, with both partners trapped in a dance of needing each other while simultaneously pushing each other away. Despite the ongoing turmoil, neither of them could break free. It felt as though they were tethered to one another by invisible threads – each experiencing the same emotional highs and lows, unable to find peace.

Over time, Sarah began to recognize the patterns playing out in their relationship. Her need for validation from David reflected the emotional neglect she had experienced as a child. She realized she was seeking approval from him in ways that she had never received from her parents. Similarly, David came to understand that his emotional withdrawal was not just a defence mechanism – it was rooted in his own unresolved fear of abandonment.

The realization that they were caught in a Karmic cycle was both painful and enlightening. Sarah and David began to see their relationship not as a source of endless pain, but as an opportunity for deep healing and self-awareness.

After a particularly intense argument, Sarah and David decided to part ways. Though painful, the separation marked the beginning of a healing journey for both parties. During this time apart, Sarah sought therapy and began working on healing her inner child. She spent time journalling, meditating and reflecting on the root causes of her insecurities. Slowly, she learned to offer herself the love and validation that she had always sought from others.

David, too, took the time to explore his emotional wounds. He confronted his fear of rejection and worked on building emotional maturity. Through introspection, he came to understand that he could heal only by learning to trust himself and others, without fear of abandonment.

Years later, Sarah met someone new, but the foundation of her relationship was different this time. She had learned the art of self-love and emotional balance. She no longer sought validation from her partner; instead, she entered the relationship from a place of wholeness and inner peace. Likewise, David worked through his emotional blocks and eventually formed a relationship grounded in mutual respect and trust.

While their relationship had been filled with turbulence, it was also a powerful catalyst for their individual growth. The Karmic lessons they learned – about self-worth, healing old wounds and fostering healthy boundaries – prepared them both for more fulfilling and balanced partnerships in the future.

Your Inner Child Healing

The concept of the 'inner child' is not new; it's a timeless idea that acknowledges an unguarded, younger version of you that still exists within, carrying the emotions, dreams and traumas from your formative years. Whether or not you recognize it consciously, this inner child continues to shape your adult thoughts, behaviours and emotional responses.

On the Twin Flame Journey, reconnecting with this innocent, vulnerable part of yourself is crucial. Over time, life's challenges, societal pressures and personal beliefs can obscure or suppress this aspect of who you are. By reconnecting with your inner child, you can access a well of creativity, joy and spontaneity – qualities that often fade with age. More importantly, this reconnection is essential for healing past wounds and reclaiming parts of yourself that may have been overlooked or forgotten.

Embracing your inner child opens the door to heart healing. This part of you holds the key to understanding past emotional pain and can guide you towards greater self-compassion, forgiveness and awareness. Healing your inner child is a journey of unlearning old patterns, revisiting your true desires and needs and cultivating unconditional self-love.

Many of us mistakenly believe that childhood is something we leave behind, suppressing memories or downplaying the significance of early experiences. However, the truth is that childhood is never truly 'over'. The inner child lives on within your heart, continuing to influence your relationships, behaviours and emotional responses. By healing this aspect of yourself you can erase the marks of past hurt and step into your full potential – whole, integrated and aligned with your authentic self.

Reconnecting with your inner child isn't about reliving the past or getting stuck in old pain. It's about reclaiming the innocence, creativity and joy that were once natural instincts for you. It's about nurturing the part of you that needs to feel safe, valued, supported and loved.

Exercises to Connect with Your Inner Child

Reconnecting with your inner child is a process and easier for some than others, depending on whether your early years were nurturing or otherwise. Below you will find some tried and tested exercises to help you begin to re-establish a nurturing connection with your inner child. These activities will allow you to reawaken forgotten aspects of yourself, heal old wounds and start to rebuild a loving relationship with this essential part of your soul. In many ways, it is the process of learning to parent yourself or growing up again – but this time with unconditional love for yourself.

Write a Letter to Your Inner Child

Sit in a quiet space and close your eyes. Imagine meeting your younger self – whether aged three, five, or any other age that feels significant. See the child clearly in your mind's eye. Begin by writing a letter to this version of you, offering words of love, comfort and understanding. Allow yourself to express the thoughts and feelings you may have been unable to share back then. This exercise can help you process unresolved emotions and foster a deeper connection with your inner child. What would you want to say to your younger self? What kind of reassurance would your child need? How would you comfort them in their times of fear or sadness?

Create a Safe Place for Your Inner Child

In your mind's eye, imagine a place where your inner child feels completely safe, secure and loved. It could be a garden, a secret room, or anywhere you feel free from the constraints of adulthood. Visualize this space in as much detail as possible, allowing all your senses to be engaged. What does it smell like? What sounds are there? What colours do you see? You may even choose to imagine toys or objects that bring comfort to your inner child in this space.

Whenever you feel overwhelmed or disconnected, you can return to this safe place for reassurance. It's a sanctuary where your inner child can rest and receive the unconditional love they deserve.

Revisit Childhood Joys

Take some time to reconnect with activities that brought you joy as a child. Whether it's drawing, dancing, playing outside – anything that made you feel light-hearted – engage in these activities without worrying about how 'productive' they are. Simply focus on the act of play. To get going right away, perform some skipping – not with a rope but the skipping you used to do as a child instead of walking. Notice how it makes you feel. Notice how your energy shifts and what emotions come up for you. This practice allows you to access the playful, creative energy of your inner child and reminds you that joy is not just something for the past – it's still available to you now. What was one thing you loved to do as a child? How does it feel to engage in this activity again? What does it bring up for you emotionally?

Lullaby Affirmations

Affirmations are a powerful tool to rewire unhealthy perceptions and nurture and heal your inner child – because believe it or not, your brain believes what you tell it. Every night before you go to sleep, when your mind is most receptive to suggestion, take a moment to speak out loud or with your thoughts to your inner child with kindness and compassion. Use lullaby affirmations such as:

'You are loved just as you are.'
'It's safe for you to express your feelings.'
'I am here for you, and I will protect you.'
'You are enough, and you always have been.'

As you speak these affirmations, place your hand on your heart or hug yourself and imagine sending love and warmth to your younger self, embracing them with all the tenderness you have within you. The more you affirm your inner child, the more you reinforce their inherent worth and begin to heal old wounds.

This journey to connect with your inner child is a sacred one. It's about rediscovering the magic, wonder and spontaneity that have always resided within you. Through these simple exercises, you are not only healing old wounds but also strengthening your capacity for joy, creativity and love. The more you nurture and parent your inner child, the more you will discover the depths of your true self – someone who is worthy of love, compassion and the full expression of life – and the closer you will move towards your longed-for Divine Union.

Karmic Bonds Vs Twin Flames: Key Differences

In summary, Karmic relationships are meant to bring unresolved emotional wounds, often tied to your abandoned inner child, to the surface for healing. They push you to confront and resolve deep-seated pain, enabling growth. On the other hand, Twin Flame relationships are about conscious awareness and higher consciousness – mirroring each other's potential for spiritual elevation. In these relationships, there is no need to 'fix' or 'parent' one another, because both individuals are already whole. The focus is not on dependency or validation, but on sharing a transformative energy that propels both towards greater spiritual alignment.

Karmic relationships are often marked by emotional instability, dependency and imbalance, leading to cycles of tension and challenge. Twin Flames have this intensity too but are characterized by mutual respect, unconditional love and the recognition that each person is already whole and complete on their own. They build each other up, rather than relying on one another for validation or emotional support.

Understanding how Karmic relationships differ from Twin Flames allows you to approach your Karmic bonds – whether current or past – with greater awareness, turning them into stepping stones for personal and spiritual growth.

No matter how complex or challenging a Karmic relationship may be, please don't regret that it happened. It is never a wasted experience. Every shade of love offers you valuable lessons, helping you become wiser and more attuned to your higher self on your Twin Flame Odyssey. Your heart is like a muscle; the more you use it or break it down with regular workouts, the stronger it gets. And, as you will see in the 'Unrequited Love' chapter (see page 219), a broken heart is the most powerful workout that your heart can ever get. It can emerge from the experience stronger, wiser and bigger.

The False Flame Relationship

If your heart gets a workout from those Karmic relationships, it can be left feeling utterly disorientated and bereft by this next category of intimate relationships on your Twin Flame Path. Welcome to the gaslighting games of the False Flame.

False Flames are one of the most heart-wrenching relationship experiences. However, unlike Karmic bonds, which can return every time you neglect your inner child, if you learn lessons from False Flame relationships and take measures to protect yourself from experiencing them again, they are something you can swerve in the future.

A False Flame may initially appear to be your perfect match – someone who understands you on a deep level and seems to absolutely adore you in a way you have never been adored before. But, as time passes, you may find yourself caught in a cycle of confusion, emotional highs and painful lows and lashings of self-doubt. False Flames are often mistaken for true Twin Flames because they mirror the same love language that characterizes genuine Spiritual Mirrors. But a surefire marker you are barking up the wrong relationship tree is that after the initial high, False Flame relationships don't create a positive shift for you or ignite a sense of purpose within you. Quite the opposite. They leave you feeling utterly lost and demeaned.

The Pattern of the False Flame

There is often a pattern to False Flame relationships, but all too often you can only recognize that pattern in hindsight, when you are licking your wounds, rather than during the emotional turmoil they bring. This section will give you an overview to help you recognize the signs of a False Flame relationship sooner rather than later and, more importantly, show you how these painful encounters can still serve as transformative opportunities.

In the beginning, the relationship feels heaven-sent. Your False Flame may shower you with unconditional praise, affection and admiration. You connect on every level, sharing your deepest thoughts and feelings. But a few days, weeks or months after this euphoric love-bombing phase, subtle signs of inconsistency emerge. Your False Flame may promise to call but disappear or ghost you without explanation. Small criticisms or hurtful comments surface. You will be told you are putting pressure on them. At first, you may brush it all off, thinking it's just a misunderstanding or that they are under stress.

Soon, though, the pattern becomes undeniable. They repeatedly use silent treatment or withdraw emotionally or physically, leaving you wondering what on Earth went wrong. You find yourself apologizing for things that aren't your fault, chasing after their affection because you recall how good it felt in the beginning and trying to maintain a connection that feels increasingly one-sided. The worst part? They always seem to leave you with just enough breadcrumbs – an occasional text or brief reconnection or half-hearted apology – to keep you hooked, hoping against hope things will snap into place.

These relationships can trigger feelings of anxiety, depression and confusion but also euphoria, making it seem as though you cannot live without their affection. Yet, despite the highs and moments of fierce intimacy, the relationship ultimately leaves you drained.

False Flame relationships are dramatically on the increase as they lend themselves particularly well to online romance scams. The TV series *Love Rats* showcases stories of False Flame relationships, many of which begin online. The 'love rat' targets someone deeply vulnerable who is rich in empathy and has a strong desire to love and be loved in return, but who is lacking in self-love and self-awareness. The love rat finds out everything about that person, makes themselves indispensable emotionally, bombarding them daily with loving texts and concern, and then moves in for the kill, exploiting their need to be loved to the full, often depleting their bank accounts and destroying their lives. It is heartbreaking viewing but highly educational and can help you identify the red flags of a False Flame and avoid these relationships. Unlike Karmic bonds, which are unavoidable as all of us must work on remembering our inner child in some way, the pain of False Flame relationships can be sidestepped – because if you are coming from a position of self-worth, the False Flame's flattery will feel inauthentic and their gaslighting won't work.

If you have succumbed to a False Flame relationship in the past, please don't beat yourself up. You are a human being, and it is in the darkness that the stars can shine at their brightest. Be compassionate to yourself always; and understand and heal the reasons why you let them into your heart and your life, so you are never a target again. The more self-compassionate and self-aware you are, the more you False Flame-proof yourself. I will now share my personal story, to show you how easy it can be for anyone to fall prey to a False Flame.

Fifteen years into my marriage, a False Flame unexpectedly appeared in my inbox. This wasn't a traditional romantic affair, but a deeply emotional, intense online connection – one that almost felt like fate. The person swept me off my feet, flattering me with beautiful words, seemingly matching me in every way. Our astrology signs were perfectly aligned, our passions mirrored each other. It was a connection that felt near-supernatural – until it didn't.

This False Flame was not all it seemed. The relationship quickly unravelled, revealing the darker side of this person, and it exposed how much I was still lacking in self-awareness and self-love. Had I truly valued myself, I would have recognized the warning signs of love bombing much sooner.

Though this emotional but not physical affair put a significant strain on my marriage, somehow my relationship with my husband survived. The respect we shared for each other, and the love we both felt for our children, kept us intact. But that heartstopping experience was an eye-opener. It made me realize that my marriage, though full of love, wasn't the perfect 'made in heaven' union we had both imagined it to be and that 'work' needed to be done.

Besides practising extreme self-care, the best way to protect yourself from love rats and False Flame relationships is to recognize the signs and end the relationship when they emerge.

15 Red Flags of a False Flame Relationship

1. **Constant drama.** Emotional highs and lows, frequent conflicts.
2. **Feeling drained.** Interactions leave you feeling exhausted instead of uplifted.

3. **Unhealthy boundaries.** They push limits or seek to control aspects of your life.
4. **You're 'fixing' them.** You're constantly trying to change or rescue them or they are trying to do the same to you.
5. **Inconsistent behaviour.** Words don't match actions; the False Flame is often unreliable or distant.
6. **Overwhelming intensity.** The relationship escalates too quickly, feeling like a whirlwind.
7. **Gaslighting.** They make you doubt your feelings or reality.
8. **Uncertainty.** You're always unsure of where you stand with them. Like walking on eggshells.
9. **Love bombing.** There's intense affection early on, but it fades once you're invested.
10. **Loss of yourself.** You neglect your interests, friends, or passions.
11. **Poor communication.** Shallow, defensive conversations; no openness.
12. **Jealousy/control.** Excessive possessiveness or attempts to isolate you.
13. **You feel worse.** Your self-esteem drops and you feel less than enough.
14. **Repetitive cycles.** Toxic patterns repeat with no real progress.
15. **Disregarding your needs and time.** Their needs and time always come first.

If two or more of the above red flags apply, you are interacting with a False Flame. Never has it been more important for you to carry on with that self-care work. The more self-love you have, the less empty you will feel and the less likely it is that you will fall for their love scam. Your heart will immediately register when their words do not match their actions and intuitively sense that their flattery of you is entirely insincere and self-serving. And along with that self-love, you need to be working on your self-awareness. While Karmic bonds shine the spotlight on your neglected inner child, False Flame relationships shine the spotlight on your shadow side (the hidden, unconscious part of your personality, which will be discussed shortly – see page 84). Until you acknowledge, face, understand and have compassion for your shadow side, your heart is left wide open for a False Flame to walk right in and create chaos.

Case Study: Julia's Journey with a False Flame

Julia, a recently divorced woman in her mid-fifties, met someone online who seemed to be everything she had ever dreamed of. His words were sweet and comforting and the connection was immediate. He told her that she was 'the one' and seemed to understand her better than anyone ever had. For weeks, they communicated nonstop. They talked about everything – her childhood, her dreams, her deepest fears – and she felt seen, heard and loved in ways she never had before.

But then the cracks started to appear. He would disappear for days without explanation. At first, Julia convinced herself that he was just busy, perhaps dealing with work stress. But as time went on, his behaviour became more erratic. He would accuse her of overreacting when she expressed concern and then make her feel guilty for questioning his love. He would disappear for longer periods, only to return with sweet messages, drawing her back in. Julia, unsure of what was happening, kept apologizing, thinking that somehow it was her fault.

As the relationship progressed, Julia found herself emotionally and financially drained. She spent her days anxiously waiting for his messages and making excuses for his absence and lack of available cash to pay for any of their dates. Her sense of self began to erode as she clung to the hope that if she loved him enough, he would love her back the same way. Ultimately, the relationship ended suddenly, when Julia discovered he had a secret life independent of her and was 'happily' married with two children and several grandchildren, leaving Julia feeling broken and confused.

In hindsight, Julia recognized that her emotional neediness, stemming from unresolved issues in her past, had made her an easy target for someone who thrived on emotional manipulation. Her lack of self-love and awareness allowed her to be drawn into this toxic dynamic.

Julia's experience exemplifies the emotional rollercoaster that many people face in False Flame relationships. She was deeply vulnerable to their charms and emotional manipulation, unaware that her shadow side – her repressed feelings of insecurity and resulting lack of self-worth – were drawing her into this painful and inauthentic dance.

A Word About Narcissists

If you are thinking False Flame relationships echo 'relationships' between narcissists and co-dependents or people who enable them, you are along the right lines. Not all False Flame encounters involve a narcissist ensnaring the heart of a trusting, gentle soul, but many do. If you are ever unfortunate enough to be caught in a narcissist's web and they have become the sole source of your validation, there must be only one mantra for you right now and that is *Self-love, self-love, self-love.* The only way to liberate your heart is to fill it right up with compassion for yourself first. Then, when you have tended to that inner wound, self-awareness must follow. Shadow work is one of the most effective ways to increase your self-awareness and to make sure that you never fall victim to the mind and heart games of a False Flame or narcissist again.

The Shadow: Embracing the Unseen Parts of You

The shadow is the unconscious part of your personality that contains repressed emotions, desires and instincts. These are the instinctual parts of yourself that you do not wish to acknowledge or express in your waking life, often because they are deemed socially or personally unacceptable. It might manifest as repressed anger, jealousy, fear of abandonment, or even unexpressed desires for power, sex or control, but often it manifests as a desire to be noticed or 'worshipped' unconditionally by someone else. These hidden parts of you are not inherently bad or wrong; they are simply aspects of yourself that you have either been conditioned to suppress or have not yet come to terms with or understood how to manage.

When you are in a False Flame relationship, your shadow side is begging for your attention, awareness and compassion and it becomes essential to acknowledge and understand this hidden part of yourself and what it is trying to tell you. Until you do, you will continue to be vulnerable to relationships that exploit your unmet emotional needs and make you susceptible to insincere flattery.

It is important to note that the shadow is not the villain here. It can be the wounded hero waiting for you to acknowledge it. Just because you feel something 'bad' does not mean you *are* bad. You are not your emotions or your thoughts. You are your choices. And False Flame relationships come into your life to show you that your shadow side should not be denied or feared but understood better. When it is repressed, you will be unable to make the best choices for yourself and others because you will be coming from a place of limited self-awareness. Indeed, you may be repressing things that are important for your personal growth. For example, if you have been told from a young age to be seen and not heard, you may have repressed your assertiveness, but assertiveness is an essential life skill in the adult world. This is your golden shadow.

Reconnect with Your Shadow

Here are exercises to help you reconnect with your shadow side. Often your shadow side simply wants you to acknowledge its existence and when you do, it loses its power. When it is repressed or denied it becomes frightening and turns needy and ugly, making you vulnerable to needy and ugly relationships.

Shadow Journalling

Spend ten minutes every day writing about your suppressed emotions. Allow yourself to express feelings without judgment. Write as if no one will read it. What emotions or traits do you find difficult to accept in yourself? Are there any past experiences or conditions that have led you to repress certain feelings or desires? How do these hidden aspects manifest in your current behaviour or relationships? What can you learn from so-called 'negative' emotions? Can you transform them? For example, if you feel envy, transform it into inspiration. If you feel anger, transform it into purpose. If you feel fear, transform it into excitement, and so on.

Shadow Dialogue

Engage in a conversation with your shadow, or those parts of yourself you try to mask. Write a dialogue between yourself and your unconscious self. Allow the shadow to speak freely and listen to what it shares with you without judgment. Have compassion for your shadow, as often it represses things with the very best of intentions to protect you. Let your shadow know that you are grateful for its help but that you don't need that level of protection anymore. You've got this.

Emotional release. When you feel anger, fear, or other difficult emotions arise, let them out in a healthy way – whether through physical exercise, creative expression, punching a cushion or simply allowing yourself to cry and cathartically release them.

Meditation. Practise meditations that cultivate self-compassion, like the guided one below. Focus on forgiving yourself for past mistakes, acknowledging your shadow and accepting your imperfections.

Guided Meditation for Self-Compassion and Coming to Terms with Your Shadow

This guided meditation encapsulates the shadow-work exercises above. Find a comfortable seat or lie down in a quiet space. Gently close your eyes and take a moment to settle into your body. If your time is limited set a timer for ten minutes. Let go of any distractions and bring your attention fully to this moment.

Begin by taking a deep breath in through your nose, allowing your belly to rise. Exhale slowly, letting go of any tension or stress. With each breath, feel more rooted, grounded and present. Imagine the Earth supporting you, providing a sense of stability and safety. Scan your body from head to toe, softening any areas of tension as you exhale. Let your body settle into a calm, peaceful state.

Picture or think about a warm, soft light at the centre of your chest, representing your inner compassion. With each breath, see this light grow stronger and brighter, filling you with love and acceptance.

Allow this light to expand, wrapping you in a gentle, comforting hug. Repeat to yourself in your mind or out loud:

> 'I am worthy of love and acceptance, just as I am.'
> 'I hold myself with compassion, no matter what I discover about myself today.'

Feel these words sinking deeply into your heart, reinforcing your ability to show yourself compassion for previous mistakes made or for feeling and thinking things that make you uncomfortable.

Gently bring your awareness to the parts of yourself that you may have hidden or denied – the shadow aspects. Imagine them as soft, distant shapes or figures, waiting to be acknowledged. With an open heart, invite these aspects of yourself to step forward. Ask these parts of yourself what they need or wish to say. Without judgment, simply listen. Trust that whatever arises is a message for your healing.

If emotions come up, listen with compassion and allow them to flow without resistance. Picture yourself gently embracing these shadow aspects with the light of your heart. Let them soften in the warmth of your compassion. Say to yourself:

> 'I see you. I accept you. You are understood.'

Feel the shift as these parts of you are surrounded by love and acceptance.

If any self-criticism or guilt arises, gently offer forgiveness to yourself. Say:

> 'I forgive myself for the times I've turned away from these parts of me. I offer myself love and grace.'

Imagine the light in your heart merging with the shadow aspects of yourself, forming a beautiful balance. You are not just light or dark – you are both, and that makes you whole. Feel gratitude for the healing that is taking place within you. There can be no day without night to define it.

Bring your attention back to your breath. With each inhale, feel grounded and calm. With each exhale, release any remaining tension. Know that you can return to this place of self-compassion and integration anytime.

After the meditation, you may want to journal or reflect on how you feel. Consider these questions: What part of yourself did you encounter today? How did it feel to show compassion to that aspect? What one small action can you take today to continue embracing yourself with love?

Glowing in the Darkness

Shadow work is a deeply transformative and sometimes uncomfortable process, but it is important on your Twin Flame Path. It is in the darkness that real growth happens. Just as the richness of the soil helps seeds to sprout, so your inner growth often comes from facing and embracing the shadows within you. When you feel conflicted or heartbroken, think of it as growing pains. You are about to learn and grow. That is something to get excited about, not to fear.

By facing, understanding and working with your shadow, you will find the strength to break free from toxic relationship patterns. You will develop a deeper understanding of yourself and your emotional needs, which will allow you to make better choices in love and life. You will also become immune to future False Flame encounters.

False Flame relationships can be devastating, but they are also powerful teachers. They show you where your self-love, self-awareness and emotional boundaries need to be strengthened. As you embark on the journey of shadow work, here is another reminder that you are not your emotions or your past; you are your choices. Just because you think or feel something does not mean you are that something. We are all a mix of positive and negative forces. It is the forces that we choose to indulge and how we react or respond to them that makes all the difference.

Through this process, you will develop the wisdom and resilience needed to attract the genuine love you deserve – the love of a true Twin Flame, one that accepts you as you are, supports your growth and leads you to deeper union with yourself.

So, take a deep breath and acknowledge that your inner darkness isn't a curse. It holds the potential for incredible transformation. Indeed, your shadow exists only because there is a source of light to create it. Your inner light has always been there, waiting to shine through. Regard your shadow side as a source of strength and potential creativity. Understand that False Flame relationships can be opportunities to heal and grow on your Twin Flame Path, not signs of failure.

Soul Mate Relationships

Coming to terms with your inner child and shadow is seminal to your Twin Flame Path. Both are unconscious aspects of your personality that urgently need to be acknowledged for your personal and spiritual growth. Karmic and False Flame relationships offer you opportunities to do this inner work but the next category of intimate relationships – Soul Mates – offer you another stunning opportunity to evolve from the inside out. In contrast to Karmic and False Flame relationships, which tend to be painful, complex and short term, Soul Mate relationships have their challenges and complexities but are more likely to be life-enhancing, simplistic and enduring. This is because Soul Mate relationships love to bring harmony and balance to two other unconscious aspects of your personality that demand your attention: your persona and your anima/animus.

The Persona and Anima/Animus

The persona is the part of you that you present to others, or the role you play in life. If you are familiar with astrology (see Chapter Four), it is akin to the rising sign, the mask you wear. It is also the part of you that is shaped by the expectations of others, or who you think you should be to be accepted or to fit in. In many cases, a Soul Mate will be someone who ticks not just your relationship expectations but also the expectations of your family and society. And you will tick all their boxes in the same way.

The anima/animus represent the traditionally masculine and feminine aspects within. Everyone is born with the potential for both sets of gender characteristics, but in most cases one set is developed consciously and in line with family expectations and social conditioning. Soul Mate relationships will either help you confirm your conscious gender expectations or encourage you to find a healthier balance within yourself between those gender characteristics.

Soul Mate relationships can have an enchanted quality. They reflect to you what you feel love should be or what family and society tell you love is. Often, Soul Mates will come from similar backgrounds, or they will share the same interests and beliefs. For the most part, connecting to them is easy; and they can feel like a match made in heaven because they meet the approval of other people in your life. You have found your forever love. Sometimes things may feel a little off, but you convince yourself nothing in life is perfect and personal compromise is what makes relationships tick, isn't it?

Soul Mate relationships make you feel comfortable, at home and safe. If you believe in reincarnation, you may meet them again and again in each lifetime. You know the role you must play in a Soul Mate relationship; and even if it doesn't always make your heart sing, or give you everything you need and want, or there are some things about your partner you would like to change, it looks right from the outside in – and sometimes that is enough.

Case Study: Soul Mate Connection

Gabriel had long struggled with self-worth, seeking external validation through relationships. Emily was highly intellectual but disconnected from her emotions, fearing vulnerability. They met at a creative retreat and quickly felt a deep connection, sharing similar family and educational backgrounds and career aspirations, but their relationship soon triggered unconscious patterns that forced both to confront and integrate aspects of themselves.

For Gabriel, his relationship with Emily challenged his 'caretaker' persona, helping him realize that his worth was not tied to being in a relationship. He began seeing his empathy as a super power and to understand the importance of expressing his own emotional needs and to set boundaries in a loving relationship. Emily, on the other hand, had built her identity around her career, avoiding emotional engagement. Gabriel's emotional openness pushed her to confront her own fear of vulnerability, helping her realize that emotional availability was a form of strength and creativity rather than a weakness.

The relationship forced both individuals to directly face their deeper fears: Gabriel's fear of abandonment and Emily's fear of emotional overwhelm. Over time, Gabriel learned to value himself independently, while Emily learned to balance her intellect with emotional presence.

Ultimately, Emily and Gabriel's Soul Mate relationship catalysed their personal growth. Their connection deepened over the years as they slowly but surely learned to love and support each other from a place of mutual authenticity and self-awareness.

Your Heart, Your Soul

Soul Mates are true to their name. They come into your life to walk beside you, hold your hand and support and enhance your soul growth like a loving best friend. They are relationships that can stand the test of time because spending time together is comforting and healing, offering you a window to find harmony between the person you are and the person others expect you to be. Although they can often be for life, sometimes they only last a season; and in contrast to a Twin Flame relationship, which is one and only, you can have several Soul Mates in your lifetime. When a Soul Mate relationship ends, it has simply run its course; this is entirely natural and to be compared to the glorious sight of autumn leaves falling from trees. Life and love lessons have been learned, and it is time for you both to move on with beauty and with grace.

I've shared my experiences with Karmic and False Flame relationships, so now I will share my experience of a Soul Mate relationship. I met him on the cusp of my thirties. Unlike the intensity of a Karmic bond, this relationship was balanced, kind and full of care. It showed me that love didn't have to be painful and dramatic. It could be steady, calm and grounded. Yes, dear reader, I married him. And after all these years, we are still together. But even our Soul Mate connection had its own unfolding.

When my husband and I first met, we offered each other what we needed at the time: balance, grounding, emotional safety and the ability to fulfil our mutual desire for starting a family. But what we didn't realize, as so many couples don't, was that a lasting, fulfilling partnership requires more than just mutual love and respect and shared life goals. It requires a commitment to each other's personal and spiritual growth.

For years, we worked to empower our marriage. I focused on self-care, boundary-setting and fulfilling my emotional needs independently and he worked on opening emotionally. But in 2017, life – as it often tends to do – threw us an unexpected curveball. My husband suffered a severe brain injury that caused irreversible memory loss and cognitive impairment. Overnight, I was thrust into the role of primary caregiver – a role I was entirely unprepared for. Before this, my husband had been in the role of protector and supporter, but now I had to step into that role for him. The process has been and remains tremendously challenging, but in it I have learned to become self-reliant, to offer unconditional love to someone vulnerable and to be patient with the unfolding of my own Twin Flame Journey.

Calling in Your Soul Mate

Soul Mate relationships can offer you a priceless opportunity to become a more balanced, authentic version of yourself who can naturally attract a partner who complements you. The reflection exercise below will help increase your chances of attracting your Soul Mate or Soul Mates into your life.

Look Into Your Eyes

Stand in front of a mirror and look into your own eyes. Study their unique beauty as windows of your soul.

Then acknowledge the parts of yourself that you consider traditionally 'masculine' and 'feminine'. This can include traits like logic (masculine) versus intuition (feminine), or assertiveness (masculine) versus receptivity (feminine).

Now, imagine each of these qualities as distinct energies within you. Close your eyes and begin to feel the masculine energy within your body – perhaps as a strong, grounded presence in your feet or chest. Then feel the feminine energy – perhaps as a fluid, open sensation in your heart or abdomen.

Focus on these energies, letting them dance within you for a few minutes. How does it feel to allow the energies to merge? How does your sense of self shift as you balance the masculine and feminine within?

Then open your eyes and look at them in the mirror from the point of view of your Twin Flame, who can see beyond your persona, or the mask you wear, and into the heart and soul of you. Someone who can see you, what is authentic and real about you and not what others might expect you to be.

Then place your hands over your heart and imagine a radiant light glowing from your chest. Visualize this light expanding and enveloping you in warmth and love.

Begin to focus on your heart centre. With each inhale, breathe in love for yourself; and with each exhale, release any fear or doubt about your ability to attract a Soul Mate.

As you sit in this heart-centred space, silently affirm:

'I am whole and complete within myself. I am ready to share my love with another.'

Sit in this reflecting space for as long as you need to. Feel the presence of your Soul Mate as if they are already with you. Then, when you are ready, take a few deep breaths and return to your day.

Embrace What You Reject in Others

Karmic, False Flame and Soul Mate relationships often reflect to you the aspects of yourself you have yet to accept. The following exercise will help you recognize and integrate the aspects of yourself that you may have repressed or rejected, and how this denial is impacting your Twin Flame Journey.

Think about past relationships and identify one or more traits in your partners that you found particularly irritating or triggering.

Take some time to reflect on whether these traits are also present in you but are perhaps hidden or suppressed. For example, if you were irritated by a partner's vulnerability, perhaps you have suppressed your own vulnerability.

Write down these traits and explore why they might be triggering. Are they aspects of yourself that you have yet to integrate or accept?

Journal about the ways you can begin to embrace these qualities within yourself. What might it look like if you allowed yourself to express the opposite energy more fully? What lessons can you learn from this dynamic?

The integration of your inner child, shadow, persona and anima/animus is a lifelong process that requires patience, self-awareness, discipline and self-love, but the effort is more than worth it. As you stop identifying with what is repelling true love, you become more magnetic – not just to a Soul Mate, but to the life that you desire.

Differences Between Soul Mates and Twin Flames

As healing, comforting, heart-expanding and as helpful as Soul Mate relationships are on your journey towards wholeness, they are not Twin Flame relationships. It is easy to understand why the two are often confused and the concepts used interchangeably, because the love you feel for them is real and empowering; but nonetheless they represent a different type of relationship with different dynamics and purpose.

Your heart naturally gravitates to what it feels will enhance or complete it and this is why Soul Mates are often a case of 'like seeks like', or 'opposites attract'. Your heart loves to be in love with a Soul Mate and the opportunity to find affirmation and wholeness they offer you, but here for your easy reference are some key differences between Soul Mates and Twin Flames:

Soul Mate relationships are based on a sense of familiarity and comfort. These connections often feel harmonious and easy, like two people who have known each other forever. Soul Mates complement each other, creating a balanced, loving partnership that supports growth but without intense challenges. By contrast, Twin Flame connection is deeply healing but can also be turbulent and challenging. Twin Flames mirror each other's strengths and weaknesses, creating a dynamic where growth often involves facing painful or uncomfortable truths.

The primary purpose of a Soul Mate connection is mutual support. While Soul Mate relationships can be transformative, their focus is more about nurturing, companionship, appreciation and creating a comfortable life and/or family together. By contrast, Divine Union is less about comfort and more about awakening both individuals to their highest spiritual potential. The purpose is often seen as one of spiritual evolution, with the relationship forcing both people to let go of any lingering roadblocks and expand into a higher state of consciousness.

Soul Mate relationships tend to offer more stability and steadiness. The emotional connection is deep but not necessarily overwhelming. These relationships can have their fair share of arguments and tension but usually foster security, trust and a sense of peace. By contrast, Twin Flame relationships are so deep and raw that they can feel destabilizing at times because Twin Flames may mirror each other's vulnerabilities. However, they also mirror each other's strengths, and this can feel wildly affirming and liberating.

Soul Mate connections typically involve a smoother, more balanced union. Both individuals generally align in their life goals, values and interests, which creates a sense of mutual respect and cooperation. While there may be challenges, they tend to be manageable and are often resolved through communication and ongoing compromise. By contrast, the dynamics between Spiritual Mirrors are marked by a push-pull energy. One or both individuals may experience periods of running from and resisting the relationship, only to return after personal growth has been made. The intensity of the union can cause periods of separation, but these separations are often part of the healing process and lead to eventual reunion when both individuals have evolved enough to maintain a balanced relationship.

In summary, while Soul Mates offer comfort and emotional fulfilment and you can have many Soul Mates in your life, Twin Flames are a path to spiritual awakening, offering you a once-in-a-lifetime opportunity to rise like a phoenix from the ashes of intense challenge and transform into a higher version of yourself.

Setting Your Heart on Fire

Although a Soul Mate gives you what you need, helps you grow in self-love and self-awareness and offers you a sense of familiarity, security, support and comfort, they cannot give your heart everything it wants and yearns for. The only category of relationship that can set your heart on fire is a Twin Flame relationship.

You may decide that you are content to stay with your Soul Mate and that the work you do on self-love and self-awareness is sufficiently rewarding; in time, this may be the path to activating Divine Union within yourself rather than in a relationship. That is a perfectly sound decision and one that is yours to make. But if your heart rather than your head was making the decision, it would want far more for you than comfort and the familiar. It would remind you that a ship is safe in a harbour but that is not what a ship was built for. A ship was built to sail the seas and navigate the mystery and depths of the ocean.

In much the same way, your heart was built for you to experience all aspects of love, including the adventure of higher love. Karmic bonds, False Flames and Soul Mates help you integrate your inner child, anima/animus, persona and shadow. Indeed, the work of healing your inner child and shadow, understanding your persona and finding balance between your anima/animus is the most radical act of love you can give yourself, others and the world. As previously highlighted, Jung referred to this process as 'individuation' and it leads to becoming a unified whole, or Self – the highest aspect of your personality. This can be realized only when you have let go of fear, understand yourself and are on your way towards the unconditional love and bliss of your Twin Flame Adventure.

And the signs that your inner work has led you to a place where you are ready to meet your Twin Flame, and experience the stages of Cosmic Love, are the 'head over heels', 'deeply in love' themes of the next chapter.

3

TWIN FLAMES SIGNS AND STAGES

If you are on your Twin Flame Journey and consciously nurturing your inner world, you are in a prime position to attract and meet your Twin Flame. This higher love may manifest romantically, platonically, or within yourself. Other relationships and their challenges have played and will continue to play a key role in helping you grow in self-awareness and self-love, but your Spiritual Mirror is someone who 'sees' you for who you authentically are and by so doing reveals areas where your heart needs to course correct or continue to evolve. There will be no place for you to hide. This higher love is perfectly captured in the movie *Avatar*, when the lead characters acknowledge their shared passion for each other with the phrase, 'I see you.'

Meeting someone who perceives both your light and dark sides and doesn't flinch is a life-changing experience. Prepare yourself. Being seen so clearly – sometimes being known even better than you know yourself – is both exhilarating and shocking. If your Twin Flame is also working on personal growth, the relationship can be deeply fulfilling because they will have no desire to change, control, or fix you.

However, if personal-growth work isn't mutual, you can expect unbearable tension, agonizing arguments and energy-draining break-ups. The key difference between Twin Flames and other relationships, though, is that you continue to feel emotionally and spiritually connected even during temporary or permanent separation. The memory of your Twin Flame lingers forever in your heart, continuing to challenge you and help you grow into your higher self with or without them in your life.

This is why, even after many years or decades of welcome or unwelcome separation, the door is never entirely closed on a potential reunion. Reconnection remains possible if both of you feel emotionally and spiritually ready and the timing is right.

Loving You at First Sight

If you've watched the classic 1945 romantic movie *Brief Encounter*, starring Celia Johnson and Trevor Howard, or read *The Bridges of Maddison County* by Robert James Waller, you'll recognize the instant connection of Twin Flame meetings. From the moment you meet, your life divides into 'before' and 'after' – with no going back. This transformative encounter changes and lights you up in every way, whether the attraction is romantic or platonic.

As you interact, feelings of déjà vu intensify. You might discover you were in the same place at the same time previously, without realizing it. A deep, unspoken familiarity bonds you physically and spiritually. You won't agree on everything, but you'll share core values and have a common sense of purpose. Where you differ, discussions feel stimulating and rewarding. No masks are needed – you can be entirely authentic.

After a short time, you'll feel as if you've known this person your entire life. A strong pull emerges and you'll never grow tired of their presence. Interactions make time vanish. Each encounter leaves you feeling challenged, educated and energized. You implicitly trust them to support you completely – they would walk a thousand miles for you and you would do the same for them. They'll always tell you the truth, even when it's difficult. Twin Flames don't lie to each other.

The love is unconditional and defies conventional expectations. You can sense their feelings and thoughts without explanation – a single look can communicate everything. Sometimes you'll embody qualities they need to develop and vice versa. For example, if you're introverted, they might be extroverted. But these differences encourage your own journey to personal wholeness. There's no expectation, competition or envy, even if one of you is more materially successful than the other. You're genuinely happy for one another's successes and care deeply for each other's failures. Through good or bad times, they have your back.

This might sound too perfect, but Divine Unions are not always blissful – they're not for the faint-hearted. They take you right outside your comfort zone which is the only place for growth to happen. They do not exist to make your life easier; they exist to help you know or see yourself completely and break through barriers that prevent you from becoming your highest self. They're transformational unions designed to help you learn, grow and evolve. They can trigger intense inner conflicts, expose emotional wounds and offer surprising lessons in unconditional love. They fully expose aspects of yourself – both positive and negative – that you might prefer to ignore. They require you to be raw, honest and vulnerable and that is not always an easy thing to do. There will be trials and challenges ahead in any Divine Union, but all with the higher purpose of helping you accept and love yourself unconditionally.

Whether they are lifelong or temporary – or even, as in *Brief Encounter*, when they last only a few precious hours but leave a memory that will last a lifetime – a Twin Flame relationship will turn your life upside down. It will inspire massive changes in heart and direction. They can bring out your best and worst, pushing you far beyond your comfort zone. Make-ups and break-ups may occur, but you often find your way back to each other – physically, emotionally or spiritually.

Case Study: Lea and Ethan

Lea was not looking for a relationship but was open to a deeper connection. One rainy afternoon, she visited her favourite bookstore and, while reaching for the same book as someone else, her hand brushed against another's. Looking up, she met Ethan's gaze – something about his eyes felt familiar, as if she had known him for a lifetime.

They spent hours talking, easily slipping into a conversation that felt effortless and intimate. Despite them having only just met, Lea felt completely at ease, like she could be her true self without pretence. Ethan seemed to feel the same way. Their shared interests, life experiences and mutual understanding created an undeniable connection.

When it was time to leave, Ethan smiled and said, 'I think we're supposed to meet again.' Lea knew, deep in her heart, that this wasn't a chance encounter but a meaningful moment of recognition.

They continued to meet over the following weeks and the bond between them intensified. Their connection was unlike anything Lea had ever known – intense, transformative and spiritual. They grew together, shedding old patterns and embracing a new, more authentic version of themselves.

From their first meeting, Lea knew: Ethan was her Twin Flame. And in his eyes, she saw that he knew it too.

Platonic Twin Flames

Twin Flame relationships are often believed to be entirely romantic, but they can be experienced platonically – and much more attention should be paid to the opportunities for personal transformation offered by these platonic Divine Unions, so that their potential for your personal and spiritual growth is not overlooked.

It may surprise you to know that your Twin Flame is not actually meant to be the love of your life. They can be, but that is not their primary function. Their purpose is to bring intensity and authenticity into your life and to shine a spotlight on your strengths and your doubts so you can then deal with and heal them yourself. They appear in your life to nudge you in the direction of unconditional love for yourself and others.

This is why they can often be so like you and mirror your own insecurities while simultaneously challenging and bringing out the best in you.

Platonic Twin Flame relationships could be with a teacher or mentor who inspires you to excel, or a friend or colleague who completely changes you for the better during a turbulent time in your life. When you encounter someone who exposes or mirrors unhealed frequencies within you, and this mirroring helps you understand yourself better and find inner healing, please pause and give thanks. This is a platonic Divine Union at work.

Case Study: Alice and Alex

Alice had always valued deep, meaningful connections but never believed she would experience one with anyone outside of her romantic relationships. That changed one afternoon, when she met Alex at a workshop on personal growth. From the moment they spoke, Alice felt an inexplicable familiarity, as though they had known each other for years.

Alice and Alex's conversation flowed effortlessly, and they found themselves in sync, sharing similar values and philosophies about life. Although their connection wasn't romantic, there was an undeniable pull between them, a recognition that went beyond mere friendship. It was as if their souls had met before and they were now simply picking up where they had left off.

As the weeks passed, Alice and Alex continued to meet, discussing their personal journeys and supporting each other's growth. Alice felt understood in a way she never had before – without judgment, only acceptance. She realized that Alex was helping her see parts of herself she had overlooked, much like a mirror reflecting her true essence.

Though their bond remained strictly platonic, Alice knew that meeting Alex was a moment of deep soul recognition. They had come together not to fulfil each other's romantic desires, but to challenge, support and inspire each other's personal and spiritual growth as Twin Flames in the truest, non-romantic sense.

What If Your Twin Flame Is a Family Member?

Many people are familiar with the idea of their Twin Flame being a romantic partner, and we have just discussed how they can be someone with whom you share a deep, intense platonic connection – for example, a friend, colleague, or mentor. But what if your Spiritual Mirror isn't a romantic or platonic partner? What if it's someone within your own family?

The notion that your Twin Flame could be a family member is often met with alarm and scepticism, but when you examine the essence of Cosmic Love you can see that it is never limited by conventional definitions or boundaries. The bond is a deep spiritual resonance that can exist romantically, platonically and within a family relationship.

A gentle reminder here that the Twin Flame Path is about inner healing, mutual transformation and spiritual growth. Your Twin Flame does not complete you but challenges you to confront your deepest desires and wounds and know yourself fully for the very first time. The connection is intense and magnetic because it exposes the truth – both the light and the darkness – within you. The energetic resonance this person shares with your soul is the key to its Twin Flame identity. A family member, such as a parent, sibling, or even a child may trigger this soul growth, expose unresolved issues, offer lessons in acceptance, love and forgiveness and guide you towards self-awareness or the revelation of your authentic or true self.

Family relationships typically fall into the Karmic bonds category of relationships in that they are relationships charged with emotions that can bring unresolved or unhealed patterns or mindsets from childhood to the surface and in so doing help you mature. They also offer an opportunity for you to break destructive Karmic patterns. A family member can, however, be a Twin Flame if they trigger seismic personal and spiritual transformation within you. For example, a sibling who challenges your need for independence, encouraging you to find a balance between rebellion and the community of your family. Or perhaps a child who mirrors your own inner struggles and awakens you to your own deep need for inner self-love and compassion.

As mentioned above, Twin Flames do not exist to make your life easier – they exist to help you break through your unconscious roadblocks so you can become your true authentic self and understand the nature of unconditional love for yourself and another person. And a family member can on occasion fulfil that role just as powerfully as a romantic or platonic relationship.

In summary, your Spiritual Mirror is someone who helps you step into your highest and most authentic self, no matter the nature of your relationship. You may decide after reading this book that you need to take the focus off the romantic idea of your Twin Flame and that a friend, teacher or family member is already serving this purpose in your life. If that is the case, welcome the life lessons and the mirror they hold up to your own soul – both the light and the darkness – knowing that this is a unique and thrilling part of your spiritual journey.

We don't talk nearly enough about the potential for family members to be Twin Flames. The same applies to the platonic Twin Flame. If you have been conditioned to think Divine Union can only be romantic, you may already have a Spiritual Mirror in your family or in your life but are failing to notice the potential markers and what this relationship offers for your personal and spiritual growth. The section below lists some of those markers – and remember, they can all apply to romantic, platonic and familial Twin Flame relationships.

Familial Twin Flame Markers

Charged emotions. You may experience intense emotions – both positive and negative – whenever you interact with this person. This can range from deep admiration and love to intense resentment and frustration.

Mirroring. The person may mirror your own world back to you, helping you become more aware of what is positive and negative within yourself and therefore leading to greater self-awareness and healing.

Unconditional love. Despite any challenge, and even when this person pushes you to the limit, you still feel an enduring bond of love and connection to them – and this love transcends physical distance and any personal conflicts.

Spiritual awakening and growth. The presence of this person in your life requires you to constantly examine your beliefs and assumptions. They may not be easy to be around at times – and if your relationship with this person is familial it will be harder to escape or separate from them than it would be in romantic or platonic connections. This person is a catalyst for your personal and spiritual growth, so if you are unable to separate from them you must constantly engage with your emotional triggers and the growth opportunities and deep healing these triggers present.

Twin Flame in Waiting

If you feel you have yet to meet your Twin Flame, there are several inner shifts and external signs that you are ready to meet them, and they are close by. If you notice some of these inner shifts listed below, get excited. You are about to begin an extraordinary adventure – and in many ways this is the most impactful phase of your Twin Flame Journey. Think of all those great love stories and movies. It is not so much the ending that engrosses you but the process of getting there, the lessons learned along the way. Right now, you are living within the beating heart of your Twin Flame Adventure. Fall in love with it every step of the way.

While each Twin Flame Path is unique, there are several common indicators that you're more than ready to encounter this powerful connection. These key points are outlined below and should be considered if you're wondering whether the time has come for you to meet your Spiritual Mirror. The more of them you experience, the closer you are to meeting your Twin Flame – either through a relationship or, for your highest good, within yourself.

A deep sense of self-awareness. Before you can truly connect with your Twin Flame and benefit from union with them, you must first come to terms with who you are at your core. This self-awareness often arrives gradually, through moments of introspection, meditation, or even painful growth periods. You begin to understand your strengths, your shadows and your desires on a deeper level. You're no longer seeking external validation; instead, you are learning to trust your inner compass. Cultivating this sense of inner wholeness is vital preparation for a Divine Union that will mirror your own growth.

Intense yearnings for something deeper. One of the clearest signs you're ready to meet your Twin Flame is not so much a yearning for an intimate relationship but a readiness for something more profound to enter your life, something beyond what you've experienced in previous relationships. This desire isn't simply for love, but for deeper meaning and purpose. Your Twin Flame offers the kind of connection that feels destined, as though there's a part of you that has been waiting for something – or someone – to reveal your soul's purpose; and that something or someone is just around the corner. This yearning or tug will encourage you to take more leaps of faith out of your comfort zone and open yourself up to new experiences.

Anticipation. Often, before you meet your Twin Flame there will be a subtle but powerful sense of anticipation in your life. You'll find yourself spontaneously pushing boundaries and embracing new routines, perspectives and ideas. You may feel as though you're expecting something to happen soon – though you don't know exactly what. This isn't the same as the anxiety or impatience; it's more of an inner knowing that something significant is coming your way. It's the kind of feeling that signals your soul is preparing for the arrival of your Spiritual Mirror; deep down, you sense that you're getting ready to step into a chapter of your life that will change everything.

A period of emotional turmoil. Many people find that before meeting their Twin Flame they encounter a period of loss, grief, transformation and serious personal challenge. It's during this period of turmoil that you come into greater alignment with your authentic self, shedding old beliefs or patterns that no longer serve your highest good. When you feel that things are going pear-shaped, it is more important than ever to trust in yourself and the universe. This is the darkness before the dawn, the labour pains before birth.

Heightened sensitivity to energy. As the time to meet your Twin Flame approaches, your sensitivity to energy may increase. You may begin to feel more empathetic to the emotions, thoughts and energies of others, especially those who are close to you. This heightened sensitivity is an indicator that your energetic frequency is shifting and expanding. You may find yourself intuitively knowing when someone is upset or when a situation is out of alignment, as your energetic sensitivity aligns with the vibrational frequency of your Divine Union.

A deep desire for union, not completion. Perhaps one of the most important signs you're ready to meet your Twin Flame is the understanding that you really do not need someone to complete you. You no longer seek to find a partner who fills a void; instead, you approach relationships with a sense of wholeness. Meeting your Spiritual Mirror is not about finding someone to fix you; it's about discovering a connection with someone who enhances your personal and spiritual growth. Your readiness is not marked by desperation for love, but by a calm and grounded openness to the transformative union that awaits.

A shift in perspective about love. As you approach the moment of meeting your Twin Flame, you may begin to view love in a new light. You realize that true love isn't about perfection or the absence of challenges or physical intimacy; rather, it's about growth, transformation, honesty and mutual support. Your beliefs about relationships may shift from a conventional view of marriage and a partner for life to a more expansive understanding of unconditional love for yourself and others as a spiritual awakening. You may start to prioritize authenticity and soul growth over superficial attraction or material or societal expectations.

A romantic relationship is no longer your top priority. While you remain open to the possibility of a romantic relationship, your happiness is no longer defined by the idea of being with or spending the rest of your life with someone. Your ongoing journey towards greater self-awareness and self-belief is fulfilling enough. You are no longer driven primarily by the search for a partner, but instead by the thrill of your own personal growth. Every morning, you'll wake up excited about who you are and who you are becoming. Your mindset is gratefully optimistic and your dreams for the future will grow bigger and more expansive.

A sense of spiritual calling or purpose. You may feel an emerging sense of purpose or calling in your life, as if something greater is beckoning you forward. This could manifest as a newfound passion for spiritual practices or creative endeavours, or a calling to contribute meaningfully to the world. The desire to meet your Twin Flame often coincides with a heightened sense of mission, where you realize that your personal growth and purpose are intertwined with the collective awakening or healing process. Meeting your Spiritual Mirror will bring you closer to this purpose, aligning both of your souls in a shared vision.

Synchronicities. The universe can speak to you in whispers and signs, guiding you along your Twin Flame Evolution with delicate, meaningful coincidences, also known as synchronicities. As you walk this sacred path, you'll discover that life is far from random – instead, it's layered with deep meaning and an intricate tapestry of connected moments, each carefully woven to lead you towards your ultimate spiritual connection, your Divine Union.

Imagine the universe as a gentle navigator, sending you subtle signals that you're precisely where you need to be on your Twin Flame Journey and that your energy is perfectly aligning with your Spiritual Mirror's. These synchronicities are more than mere chance; they are spiritual messages designed to guide, comfort and reassure you. You might find yourself unexpectedly encountering a white feather, discovering a coin with a significant date, or experiencing an inexplicable moment of perfect timing that feels too perfect to be accidental. Often you may also begin to have vivid nocturnal dreams about meeting your Twin Flame. These dreams might feel deeply comforting and illuminating. (For more insight into the power of your dreams on your Twin Flame Path, see Chapter Five.)

Numbers can become messengers of Cosmic Love. The universe communicates through master numbers 11, 22 and 33 – each carrying a unique energetic vibration. When you repeatedly see the number 11, consider it a spiritual wake-up call, a cosmic nudge alerting you to the imminent presence of your Twin Flame. The number 22 invites you to believe in yourself, to transform your dreams from ethereal wishes into tangible realities. And 33? This is the number of psychic awakenings, signalling that a profound spiritual transformation awaits you.

Indeed, any number that repeats, for example 44, 55, 66, 77, 88, 99, is believed to be a spiritual mirror sign encouraging you to tune into the vibration of that number on your Twin Flame Path. It is also believed that seeing the number 168 means that spiritual forces are urging you to focus on your Twin Flame journey, because 1 is associated with the energy of new beginnings, 6 with love and harmony and 8 with abundance.

These synchronicities, signs and vivid dreams are not random interruptions but deliberate guidance. They are the universe's love letters, written in the language of meaningful coincidence, designed to lead you towards your most authentic self and your ultimate spiritual partnership.

Your Twin Flame Awakening is unfolding exactly as it should, one synchronistic moment at a time.

Missing Your Signs

If you are under a great deal of stress or locked into difficult life circumstances it is easy to miss the indicators and signs that have the potential to guide. If this is the case for you, it is important to focus on your emotional wellbeing rather than spiritual self-help – because until you understand how you are feeling and why, you won't be able to remove anxiety-inducing roadblocks on your Twin Flame Path. Anxiety and the stress it can cause are the enemy of physical, mental and emotional health and love in all its forms.

And bear in mind that it may not be just you missing the signs: your Twin Flame may also be dealing with things in their life and not in the optimum position, personally and spiritually, to meet you in person. Be patient, trust the process and use this waiting period to help you better understand yourself and others. Your personal-growth work is never wasted.

Twin Flame Attraction Rituals

Manifesting your Divine Union is not about forcing a relationship to happen; it's about aligning with the energy of love and becoming an expression of that love. Allow your journey to develop naturally and be patient with yourself and the process. The following is a summary of spiritual techniques you can aim to use every day, starting now, to help you attract your Twin Flame. Again, the emphasis here is on the word 'attract' – you are not chasing your Twin Flame. The exercises can encourage you to focus on cultivating inner alignment and healing, creating a clear energetic pathway to attract your Spiritual Mirror.

Mirror of the Soul Meditation

Purpose: Align your energy with the Twin Flame qualities you seek to attract.

Find a quiet space and close your eyes. Focus on your breath.
Visualize a mirror reflecting not just your outer self, but your inner being too.
Write down three qualities you want in your Twin Flame and imagine them merging with your essence in the mirror.
Affirm:

'I am whole and complete. I embody the qualities I seek in my Twin Flame.'

Sit for 5–10 minutes, feeling this energy resonate within you.

A Future Love Letter

Purpose: Heal emotional blocks and align with the Twin Flame love you want to attract.

Write a love letter to your Twin Flame, expressing gratitude for their future presence and the soul connection you share.

Acknowledge any emotions or blocks that arise during writing.

End your letter with:

'I open my heart to love. I trust the universe is guiding me to reunion.'

Reflect on any emotions, allowing them to express themselves and heal.

Sacred Union Meditation

Purpose: Balance your inner reason and creativity.

Place two objects before you: one representing your inner logic (for example, something made of wood or metal) and one representing the imaginative (for example, a crystal or flower).

Sit quietly and focus on the qualities of both energies – practical (strength, logic) and profound (intuition, creativity).

Hold each object, imagining both energies flowing harmoniously within you, bringing a sense of healing and wholeness.

Write an intention:

'I welcome balance within and am open to attracting my Twin Flame.'

Sit for a few minutes, feeling the energy and inner peace when there is balance between your reason and your creativity.

Raise Your Vibration

Rather than one single technique, it is now time to implement daily changes to your life. On a regular basis, begin to consciously engage in self-care, connect with positive people and live more authentically. The more at peace from the inside out you are, the more likely you are to attract your Spiritual Mirror. (You can find in-depth practical techniques for how to raise your vibration on page 00.)

Work on Trust

Last but by no means least, be patient and open to the process. Again, this is not a single technique, but a life-long practice.

Manifesting your Twin Flame is about healing, self-love and trusting that everything will unfold naturally. Believe your

Spiritual Mirror is already out there and that the universe will bring them to you at the perfect time and in the right way for you and for them. Trust in the divine timing. Release attachment to how or when your Twin Flame will appear.

Classic Twin Flame Relationship Stages

Every Divine Union is deliciously unique. Some will last a lifetime, while others may not. Regardless of the nature and timeline of the relationship, there will be common stages, and these experiences will linger in your mind, heart and soul for a lifetime.

> **Meeting.** You may feel emotionally overwhelmed for a while after you first meet your Twin Flame, sensing your higher connection to them and that they have everything you need and want in a relationship. There may be a yearning for something more and a synchronicity or two prior to this electric meeting. For example, you may have had a dream and experience a sense of destiny especially if you meet them in unusual circumstances.
>
> **Bliss.** When you spend time together and discover just how aligned you are and just how much you have in common, you know it is a case of two becoming one. Expect to feel blissed-out.
>
> **Doubt.** After the initial glow, you may start to second guess yourself and look for problems that aren't there. It all feels too good to be true and this can lead to periods of personal doubt and insecurity.

Growth. Doubts may lead to tension and conflict and a period of unsettling ups and downs. Your partner will know your flaws and you will know theirs – and being so like each other, you must face, understand and embrace their flaws just as they must embrace yours. If that mutual growth can't happen, separation will occur.

Separation. Your partner reflects or shines a light on aspects of yourself that you feel uncomfortable with, or still need to better understand, and this reflection can lead to falling out and a period of separation to help you both process and work further on your personal growth. If your Twin Flame runs away or ghosts you, your mission is not to run after them: the decision to return must be theirs and theirs alone. It is entirely possible that their role in your life is over because they have helped you see yourself fully. Stop worrying and trying to control what you cannot control – that being someone else – and double down on your personal growth and vibration-raising work. Visualize the love you have for them. Be grateful for the time you had together and get busy focusing on other areas of your life.

You may well find that your Twin Flame returns of their own choice, but in some cases the separation will be permanent. For example, you or your Spiritual Mirror may have vulnerable dependents or live in another country, or your Twin Flame has more personal-growth work to do, or they may pass away. You then need to come to terms with the fact that your Spiritual Mirror can live only in your heart but not in your life. Acknowledge the loss and practise self-care.

Letting go in the physical sense can lead to dramatic life changes as you move forwards and find ways to transform your broken heart into something deeply meaningful.

Reunion. There may be an opportunity to rekindle the connection again in person. If they return but the work you both need to do to maintain the relationship is exhausting and the relationship doesn't feel like a safe place anymore, you may have to decide to end the physical relationship. However, this ending can be regarded as a new beginning because the relationship has activated your spiritual awakening, also described in spiritual circles as Ascension (see page 134).

Gratitude. Whether the relationship or meeting was short or long term, you recognize that meeting your Twin Flame has enlightened and empowered you and brought you an inner awareness and peace beyond understanding. Any feelings of loss, regret, resentment or guilt will subside, and you will feel nothing but gratitude that they touched and transformed your life. If the relationship has ended through irreconcilable differences or bereavement, their love has found a permanent home in your heart and their memory remains forever alive with you in spirit.

Surrender. You let go of any attachment to people and things that you think you need but that for whatever reason are not working out – and this can include your Twin Flame. The whole purpose of a Divine Union is to educate you about the nature of unconditional love and to help you transcend all boundaries and definitions you may have previously had about love. You start making decisions from a place of love and not ego.

Your ego always seeks to change others and the world around you to make you feel fulfilled, but the love inside you understands that only when you find inner peace will the world around you and your relationships change. In other words, you understand that the only person you can control is yourself. What anyone else – including your Twin Flame – thinks, feels, says or does is entirely down to them and not you. You appreciate who you are and what you have and feel gratitude for every moment. You will always send love to your Spiritual Mirror, but you don't need them in your life to complete or fulfil you. Indeed, what other people think matters less and less.

And even though your Twin Flame is the most complete, intense and magical union you will ever experience, if the relationship ends this will not be the end of your world because you have been reborn personally and spiritually by the encounter. You have learned how to take responsibility for yourself and how to align your energy with the universe, notice the signs it is always sending you and prioritize learning, growth, self-awareness and self-love. You know what it means to feel truly, madly and deeply alive and in love with life itself.

Soul Mates Are Not Twin Flames

Now that you are more aware of the Divine Union, it is helpful to remind you of what you learned in the previous chapter: that even though there are similarities between Soul Mates and Twin Flames, and though both can be loving, enduring and life-enhancing romantic connections, they are not the same thing.

The most obvious difference is that you can have only one Twin Flame, and may not even meet them in your lifetime, but you can have several Soul Mates. And even though you may feel you can be completely yourself with your Soul Mate, that you can love them passionately, that they can influence your life deeply and that when you look into their eyes the connection is familiar and strong, the chances are they won't push you to know yourself fully and awaken your soul in the extreme way that a Twin Flame will. In some ways, a Spiritual Mirror is your ultimate Soul Mate or your Soul Mate on speed. They show you the way to your highest self but also to your lowest self – the connection can be both blissful and toxic, with an addictive quality. This is why true Twin Flames can break you down before they build you back up, and why it can feel easier to stay and feel safe in a Soul Mate relationship.

When you first meet your Twin Flame the feeling is magnetic and like the attraction you feel for a Soul Mate. What will be different is the intensity with which they mirror you or help you reveal who you truly are. This is why Twin Flame relationships are often tumultuous: they can pull you apart to help you finally let go of mindsets and behaviours that no longer serve you, so that you can create a new level of awareness – and often an entirely new perspective and life direction – before you put yourself together again.

Soul Mate relationships have their ups and downs too but when the dust settles there will be an air of calmness and common sense, whereas Divine Unions are always intense and often irrational. They help you feel heard and seen and are your path to wholeness – but only if you are secure within yourself and your Twin Flame is too. If you aren't feeling secure within yourself, then the Divine Union will fail until you can find that inner self-mastery. Think of it as learning to play an instrument. You need to learn your scales and put in the practice before you can play a piece of beautiful music.

The Self-Partnering Twin Flame Union

If you have met your Twin Flame and for whatever reason can't make your relationship with them work, coping with the loss of their physical presence can prove painful. But over time you will understand the reasons for meeting them and for their departure. It was all for a higher purpose. You needed to find your own inner love and power.

You are now stronger and wiser and more fulfilled – not just because you met them and that meeting inspired a higher love within you, but also because they are now absent from your life. You understand that your Twin Flame Journey continues. Their physical absence ignited in you a longing to make every moment of your life count; and an understanding that when two people connect on a spiritual level, the physical connection can end but the spiritual bond never does.

If you're currently in the phase of waiting to meet your Spiritual Mirror and doing the inner work, which means focusing on your self-awareness and nurturing your self-love, you might well find that, over time, the longing to meet your Twin Flame in person begins to fade. This subsidence happens naturally as your personal and spiritual growth deepens, to the point where Divine Union can in some cases happen spontaneously and beautifully within you.

There is no right or wrong way to experience Divine Union. It reveals itself in the most surprising and wondrous ways, whether through a relationship or solo. Perhaps it will happen through an unexpected encounter with someone who makes your heart soar, and your soul rejoice. Or it may arise in a quiet moment of inner awakening – an epiphany that leaves you feeling both euphoric and connected on a soul-deep level to your higher self.

The mystery of *how* and *when* this union will occur is part of the magic of walking your Twin Flame Pilgrimage. The adventure is living and loving the journey itself. Once you recognize that Cosmic Love is your birthright, and that living without it is the greatest of personal and spiritual losses, the only thing left for you to do is to focus on deepening your love and understanding of yourself. In doing so, you know that your Divine Union will happen inevitably – whether within you or before you.

Don't ever think of solo Divine Union as somehow second best. It can be just as transformative, blissful and powerful as meeting your Twin Flame in person or having a full-blown relationship with them. Both paths to your higher self can lead to the same personal growth and spiritual awakening, each serving as a reflection of the Divine Union already alive within you.

Case Study: Willow's Inner Divine Union

Despite having several relationships, Willow, a 44-year-old woman, spent years feeling incomplete. She longed for something more and struggled to find lasting fulfilment. After turning to spirituality in her early thirties, Willow encountered the concept of inner Divine Union – the idea that the key to true union was the harmony of light and dark forces and balance of masculine and feminine energies within herself.

Willow was initially sceptical but began practising deep meditation and self-reflection. Over time, she realized she had neglected her feminine energy, focusing too much on external achievement and ignoring her emotional depth. As she healed and celebrated both her masculine drive and feminine intuition, a quiet shift occurred. One evening, after meditation, she felt a deep sense of inside-out peace and wholeness. She understood that the Divine Union she had been seeking was never about meeting another person who would 'complete' her – it was about finding balance and love within herself.

From that moment, Willow felt complete. She no longer sought validation from external relationships and began to live from a place of inner peace and self-love. Though open to the possibility of a partnership, she now knows that true union begins within.

An Inner Divine Union Meditation

Divine Union always begins within. The external relationship – whether romantic or not – is simply a reflection of the balance and harmony you have cultivated within yourself. When you find this union within, you are already complete and at peace – no matter what the external world brings or does not bring. To help you become receptive to your Divine Union, try this mini-meditation:

> Find a quiet space and sit or lie down comfortably. Close your eyes, take a deep breath in and exhale slowly. Let your body relax with each breath.
>
> Visualize (or describe to yourself) roots extending from your feet deep into the earth. Feel grounded, stable and connected to the Earth's energy.
>
> Bring your awareness to your heart centre. As you breathe in and out, deeply visualize a warm, golden light glowing from within, representing your true essence.
>
> Picture a golden light at the top of your head (crown chakra), representing your strength, purpose and clarity.
>
> Visualize or describe to yourself a soft, pink or silver light at your heart, representing intuition, compassion and nurturing.
>
> See these two lights slowly moving towards each other and merging in your heart. Feel their perfect balance and harmony. You are whole and complete within yourself.
>
> Silently repeat these affirmations:

'I am whole and complete within.'
'I honour and love myself unconditionally.'
'I am both strength and softness, perfectly balanced.'

Let the light in your heart expand, filling your entire body with warmth, love and acceptance.

Know that the Divine Union you seek is happening within you. You are already united with yourself – there is nothing more you need to search for.

Gently say to yourself:

'I am my own Twin Flame. I am complete and whole within.'

Imagine the light surrounding your entire being, protecting and nurturing this inner harmony. Feel the peace of knowing you are always united with yourself.

When you're ready, slowly bring your awareness back to the room. Wiggle your fingers and toes, stretch gently and open your eyes. Carry the energy of your inner Divine Union with you throughout your day.

Remember: The path to true Divine Union is first and foremost internal and energetic – starting with your thoughts, feelings and beliefs about yourself. Like energy attracts like energy. That is a law of the universe, and your internal beliefs are energy. When you feel whole again, the world around you reflects that completeness right back at you.

Get Ready

Your Twin Flame is out there in your future and the universe is pulling you towards it. To ready yourself for it, you need to understand yourself from the inside out and approach your personal and spiritual growth with renewed enthusiasm. This should never feel a chore; it should be a conscious choice you make every day.

All the advice and exercises in this book will play their part in your personal and spiritual growth and help pave the way for your Divine Union, however that will manifest. And perhaps the most significant thing you can do to prepare is to raise your vibration on every level – physically, mentally, emotionally and spiritually.

This book isn't a holistic healing manual, but you can find plenty of expert guidance online or in book form if you know deep down that more work needs to be done in any of the following areas of your life.

> Make sure your diet is as healthy as possible and that you exercise for at least 30 minutes a day, ideally outdoors in the fresh air. Take good care of your body, as the temple of your soul that it is.
>
> Be curious and openminded and learn something new as often as you can. Give your mind plenty of stimulation.
>
> Become more aware of the quality of your sleep and do all you can to optimize it.
>
> Spend less time online and avoid the blue light from screens as much as you can.

Meditate or find ways to focus mindfully on observing your thoughts and feelings without interacting with them.

Spend more time in nature. Walk barefoot in your garden if you can. Fresh air is good for you in mind, body and soul.

Listen to music that gives you goosebumps and read lots of great books.

Start and end your day with positive thoughts and actions.

Make sure you are always kind and compassionate to yourself. Become your own best friend.

Do all you can to impress the person you are becoming: your future self.

Declutter your life. Ensure your living and working spaces are tidy.

Set boundaries. Get rid of toxic relationships.

Let go and cry as often as you need to. Tears are cathartic and healing.

Learn how to manage stress and ensure you have moments of peace, quiet and calm each day. Salt baths are great for cleansing and relaxing.

As well as learning to unconditionally love yourself, learn to love falling in love with a pet, a plant, an idea or project – ideally one that helps make the world a better place. This is empowering because you can't receive what you can't give.

Dream recall. Dreaming is good for your holistic wellbeing, and it is possible to meet your Twin Flame in your dreams (see Chapter Five).

Ascension

The Twin Flame Journey is also your gateway to Ascension – a spiritual term used to describe your transition from lower, dense energy vibrations to higher, lighter frequencies. Ascension is more than spiritual awakening; it's about becoming your fullest self, embodying higher consciousness, love, peace and wisdom. It is recognizing that you are a soul having a human experience.

As you ascend, you align with your soul's divine blueprint, tapping into higher and higher aspects of consciousness. You shift from the material, ego-driven world to a spiritual realm of unity consciousness, where everything is interconnected and all are loving expressions of the same energetic source. You transcend the limitations of mind and body, elevating your energy to resonate with unconditional love for yourself and others.

A note of warning: Ascension brings significant personal changes. You may find yourself disconnecting from people who no longer align with your new energetic vibration. Longstanding relationships might fall away; if this happens, don't be discouraged – you're simply shedding old layers of yourself and mindsets, routines and relationships that no longer serve you. This transformation might even extend to your work life, where you'll seek more meaningful and rewarding opportunities.

Your tolerance for negativity will dramatically increase. Gossip, cruelty, lies, cheating and pessimism will become increasingly intolerable. Your newly enlightened self, with its raised vibration, wants nothing to do with these lower energies. Alcohol and other unhealthy routines will lose their appeal. All these changes can cause conflict with people in your life who can't keep up with your new way of seeing and doing things, but you aren't ever going back now you have seen your own light.

At its core, Ascension is about remembering your true nature – divine, infinite and energetically interconnected with all existence. You awaken to your soul's infinite potential, realizing you are more than your physical body or ego. This process involves releasing lower-vibrational states like fear, guilt and shame and embracing higher-consciousness states of love, peace and joy.

Ascension is not a destination but a continuous vibrational journey. With each step on your Twin Flame Odyssey, you move closer to your truest self and your Ascension. Nurture this process daily through heart-centred practices: meditation, gratitude, presence, connection with nature and surrounding yourself with positive influences. Practise self-care, self-compassion and positive affirmations. Treat yourself with unwavering kindness and respect.

These practices are your stepping stones, guiding you higher where your soul's light shines brightest and your purpose becomes clear. Every moment of self-awareness, every act of self-love and every positive vibrational shift moves you towards higher love, infinite peace and transcendent bliss.

Your soul has waited eternally for this moment: its greatest expansion. The universe has conspired to make it happen at a time that is exactly right for you – and when it happens it will feel entirely natural and exactly where you are meant to be.

For now, just keep on going with your self-awareness and self-love work and keep on looking up as you do – safe in the knowledge that there are no limits to the love and joy waiting for you to claim them.

4
TWIN FLAME ASTROLOGY

As the previous pages have made clear, the key to attracting your Twin Flame – or a love that evolves your soul and truly enhances your life – begins with being self-aware and authentic. Simply put, become yourself. True love can be found only when you've made peace with your inner world. This means that your inner child isn't running the show, your shadow self feels acknowledged, your persona isn't in control and your anima/animus are balanced. It's about knowing that no matter how perfect a relationship may seem on the surface, it won't bring you inner peace if you don't already have that peace within – especially when you're alone. Inner peace comes from a commitment to personal growth, from trusting your intuition and from taking full responsibility for the choices you make in your life.

When you meet your Twin Flame, you will feel a deep recognition that resonates on an energetic, spiritual level. However, while the connection is rewarding, a Divine Union isn't without its challenges. Your heart is always at the centre of the experience; and practising heart-centred rituals, as discussed in this book, will help you stay aligned with your true essence and guide you. You may nonetheless also encounter moments where you feel you need extra or more specialist support to help you navigate the complexities of your Twin Flame Odyssey.

This is where metaphysical tools, especially astrology, can play a pivotal role. When understood and applied correctly, Twin Flame astrology offers insights that can help you not only attract your Spiritual Mirror but also sustain and strengthen that connection. Astrology can guide you through challenges, helping you match and meet the cosmic energies that support your Twin Flame Journey and your personal evolution along the way.

What Is Twin Flame Astrology?

You are likely familiar with the phrase 'as above, so below'. Astrology is an ancient mystical science that believes the positioning of the stars and planets when you were born and then their progression throughout your life can influence your life and your destiny. It is easy to see how astrology might relate to your Twin Flame Journey, given the role of intimate relationships – whether Karmic, Soul Mate or Twin Flame – in helping you discover who you are and what true love is. Astrology is therefore a highly recommended tool you can use to enhance your personal and spiritual transformation.

Astrology can't necessarily tell you what sun sign your Spiritual Mirror should be, but it can indicate likely personality traits you would benefit from tuning into; and if you are already in a relationship, it can help you pinpoint areas in which you are compatible and areas that may prove challenging. It is a powerful tool for gaining deeper self-awareness and understanding the dynamics of your relationships. In much the same way that your Twin Flame reflects and reveals aspects of yourself, astrology can serve as a mirror to help you learn more about your own internal world and the connections you share with others. By studying your birth chart and the astrological positions of the planets, you can uncover valuable insights that may guide you.

You're likely familiar with your sun sign, whether that's Aries, Taurus, Gemini, or another sign in the zodiac. However, your sun sign represents only a small portion of the overall picture of who you are in astrological terms. A full astrological birth chart maps out the positions of all the planets at the exact moment you were born, offering a far more comprehensive understanding of your personality, behaviours, strengths and challenges. For those specifically interested in exploring astrology as a tool on their Twin Flame Adventure, understanding the placement of other celestial bodies in your chart – as well as your sun sign – is helpful, particularly the placement of your Venus sign, your rising sign and your North Node placement. You'll need to know your time of birth to calculate your birth chart, but you can use astrology to guide your Twin Flame Journey even if you just know your sun sign. This is because your sun sign represents your core identity, life lessons and how your higher self or soul needs to express itself for your fulfilment, which are the crucial factors when it comes to attracting and aligning with your Twin Flame.

How Your Sun Sign Helps on the Twin Flame Journey

Each sun sign offers unique insights into the lessons and challenges you'll face with your Spiritual Mirror. Here's a snapshot overview:

Aries – Teaches self-empowerment and courage.
Taurus – Guides you to build stability and devotion.
Gemini – Encourages deep communication and flexibility.
Cancer – Nurtures emotional intimacy and healing.
Leo – Promotes self-love and creative expression.
Virgo – Focuses on service, health and self-improvement.
Libra – Teaches balance and harmony in life and relationships.
Scorpio – Inspires transformation and emotional depth.
Sagittarius – Expands horizons and philosophical growth.

Capricorn – Shows the value of commitment and long-term goals.

Aquarius – Promotes innovation and soul-level connections.

Pisces – Encourages intuition, compassion and spiritual growth.

Even without your full chart, you can still use your sun sign to guide you towards inner healing and alignment with your authentic or higher self, which is key to attracting your Twin Flame. Your sun sign can also offer you essential clues about the soul lessons you're meant to learn.

However, if you do know your time of birth and can therefore access your birth chart, you might want to look a little deeper at the specifics of Twin Flame astrology.

Twin Flame Astrological Placements

In the past, if you wanted to know all the placements in your birth chart, you would typically need to consult with a professional astrologer who could calculate it for you. Fortunately, times have changed. Today, you can easily generate your birth chart for free using online calculators. Simply search for 'free astrology birth-chart calculator' and you'll find a range of tools that can produce a detailed chart for you. To use them, you'll need to provide your birth date, time and location and country of birth. Once you've entered this information, your birth chart will be instantly ready to view, giving you a clearer picture of the astrological influences that shape you.

However, there is a word of caution here. While many of these calculators are free, some may ask for your email address to send you your chart or offer additional services. It's important to be mindful of privacy concerns and avoid sharing personal information with sites that seem overly pushy or intrusive. Always take the time to review any site you use and opt out of unnecessary follow-ups or subscriptions if you feel uncomfortable.

It is often said that Twin Flames share similar sun signs or the elemental influences that rule them – fire, earth, water, or air – although this isn't always the case. While it's true that Spiritual Mirrors may sometimes share the same sun sign or ruling element, the deeper connections between their birth charts may not always be so obvious. Even pairs with seemingly incompatible signs – like Aries (a fire sign) and Pisces (a water sign) – can resonate on a vibrational level and share significant connections. The key to understanding these connections lies in exploring the full scope of both individuals' astrological charts.

Your birth chart won't ever offer a direct 'yes' or 'no' answer to the question of whether someone is your Twin Flame. However, Twin Flame astrology can provide you with valuable information about your compatibility, helping you identify areas where you might experience mutual growth as well as potential issues. By examining key astrological points, in particular your rising sign and your Venus sign, you can gain insights into the emotional and relational dynamics that are at play between you and someone else. Additionally, a deeper examination of your North Node – the point in your chart that represents your soul's purpose – may offer clues about the nature of your Twin Flame, revealing Karmic ties or shared life journeys and lessons.

In a nutshell, while astrology may not definitively tell you whether someone is your Twin Flame, or when you will meet your Spiritual Mirror if you are not in a relationship, it can certainly provide valuable guidance and insight into the direction your Twin Flame Evolution is heading in. Understanding your own birth chart and the astrological patterns it contains, along with your partner's birth chart, can help you navigate the complexities of your existing relationship and, better still, uncover opportunities for personal transformation and healing along the way.

Assuming that you have a printout of your birth chart and can see what your Venus and rising signs are and where your North Node placement is, let's consider these three specific Twin Flame astrological indicators in turn.

♀ Your Venus

You might think you already know how you want to be loved; but if you've been making relationship choices from a place of low self-awareness, you've likely been attracting partners who are not equipped to love you in the way you truly need. Exploring the placement of the planet Venus in your birth chart will give you a richer understanding of your needs in love.

Your Venus placement serves as a gateway to your heart, revealing how you express affection, what you seek in a partner and how you experience and attract love. Having an appreciation of your own needs in love is crucial, because ultimately you want a partner who can meet and validate those needs. What's even more important about Venus is that it also governs how you love yourself. It's essential to remind you that on your Twin Flame Journey you're not approaching love from a place of lack or emptiness. You understand that others cannot give you what you are meant to give to yourself. Venus therefore may hold the key to your self-healing, as it reveals the optimum way to love both yourself and others.

Venus – the planet of love, attraction, beauty and the way we connect with others on a soul-deep level – can play a particularly sacred role because it highlights your love language. By studying your own and your Twin Flame's Venus signs, you can gain insight into how your unique love story is likely to unfold. You'll also have a clearer understanding of the challenges and strengths that may arise as you merge with your counterpart.

Each of the 12 zodiac signs influences Venus differently, shaping the way love is experienced and expressed. Below you will find a breakdown of how Venus manifests in each sign, but it's important to remember that these generalizations can provide only a broad outline. You are unique, as are your relationship dynamics; so, while the placement of Venus can provide you with valuable insight and indicators, it is (like everything else) only one piece of your higher love puzzle.

♈ Venus in Aries: Bold, Passionate and Adventurous

People with Venus in Aries are full of energy and intensity, both in life and in love. Their enthusiasm is contagious, and they're naturally drawn to partners who are strong, confident and fully supportive. In relationships, they love fiercely, thriving on excitement, adventure and a bit of unpredictability.

These individuals may feel a deep connection with others who have Venus in fire signs like Leo, Sagittarius, or Aries, as there's an undeniable spark between these pairings. However, the intensity of Venus in Aries can also lead to challenges. They may struggle with impatience, a desire for constant novelty and a reluctance to compromise.

Self-Help Advice for Venus in Aries

Your passionate nature can make you eager for immediate connection and excitement but sometimes love requires patience. Instead of rushing into new experiences or constantly seeking novelty, allow relationships to deepen over time. Take the opportunity to nurture and build trust with your partner, understanding that stability is not a sign of stagnation but of strength.

You value freedom and independence in your relationships, but should not be afraid to lean into vulnerability. Wishing to maintain your autonomy is natural but try balancing this with moments of emotional closeness and trust. Relationships flourish when both partners can be themselves without fear of losing their identity.

While your strong desires and passionate nature can sometimes make compromise feel like a loss, it's important to remember that relationships require give and take. Practise being open to the perspectives of others, especially those with Venus in air signs, who can offer a more rational, balanced and detached approach to problem-solving. This doesn't mean giving up your desires; rather, it means finding ways to meet your partner halfway while maintaining mutual respect.

You thrive on excitement and can bring the same spark to everyday routines. Learn something new together. Look for the thrill in small, spontaneous moments – whether it's trying a new hobby together or exploring a new part of your city. Keeping things fresh doesn't always mean big gestures; it's about maintaining a sense of curiosity and playfulness.

With your fiery love heart, it's easy to get caught up in the heat of the moment. Practising mindfulness and emotional regulation can help you approach conflicts with calm and clarity. Take a step back before reacting impulsively and give yourself space to cool down when you feel overwhelmed. This will not only improve your relationships but also help you maintain inner peace.

♉ Venus in Taurus:
Sensual and Stable Love

Venus is right at home in Taurus, making this placement one of the most grounded and sensual expressions of love. Those with Venus in Taurus crave beauty, stability and loyalty in their relationships. Venus in Taurus often finds compatibility with those who also have their Venus placement in Taurus, or in Cancer and Libra, as these people share a similar desire for emotional depth and stability in love.

A peaceful, secure home life is essential, and physical affection plays a major role in how they connect with others. There's a strong need for harmony – both emotional and financial. However, this attachment to security can sometimes lead to a resistance to change or an overreliance on comfort and material possessions. It's important if you have this Venus placement to find balance, staying open to growth and change while still nurturing the stability you crave. At its best, Venus in Taurus offers a steady, nurturing foundation, but growth requires letting go of limiting attachments and embracing transformation.

Self-Help Recommendations for Venus in Taurus

While you value stability, it's important to invite change slowly and intentionally. Start by making small, manageable adjustments in your routine or environment to help you become more comfortable with transformation. This can open space for you to grow, both personally and within your relationships.

While comfort and material security are key, remember that true peace comes from within. Challenge yourself to let go of attachments to possessions or the idea of 'perfect' stability. Focus on cultivating inner peace and flexibility.

Venus in Taurus can sometimes lean towards complacency. Set personal goals that encourage consistency and discipline, whether that's in your career, fitness, or spiritual practice. Regular commitment to growth and exposure to new experiences will help you avoid stagnation.

Grounded as you are, it can be easy to stay in your comfort zone, but true intimacy requires emotional openness. Practise being more vulnerable with your Twin Flame and those close to you. Let your partner see your softer, more sensitive side.

While Venus in Taurus enjoys luxury and comfort, practise gratitude for the simple pleasures in life. A daily gratitude practice can help shift your focus away from materialism and towards the richness of emotional connection and the present moment.

By balancing your need for stability with a willingness to grow and evolve, you can create a more fulfilling, dynamic Twin Flame Path that nurtures both your heart and soul.

♊ Venus in Gemini: Embracing Curiosity and Connection

Venus in Gemini infuses relationships with a vibrant, curious and communicative energy. People with this placement thrive on mental stimulation and value deep intellectual connections in love. They enjoy playful exchanges, lively conversations and exploring new ideas and perspectives. However, their dual nature often leads to a wandering eye and a tendency to seek novelty in relationships.

Venus in Gemini fosters a dynamic and open relationship that thrives on variety and mental engagement. However, the desire for change and new experiences can sometimes create tension around commitment, as the push for novelty may challenge the stability required for a more intense connection. Complementary Venus signs for this placement include Gemini, Sagittarius and Aquarius, all of which share a love for intellectual connection, freedom and exploration.

Self-Help Recommendations for Venus in Gemini

Gemini's dual nature makes it easy to get swept up in the excitement of new experiences. Take the time to understand who you are outside of your relationship. Explore your passions, beliefs and desires and don't be afraid to evolve. The stronger your sense of self, the more fulfilling your connections with others will be.

While Venus in Gemini thrives on mental stimulation, remember that relationships require emotional intimacy and the reassurance of routine as well. Invest time in understanding your deeper feelings and learning how to express vulnerability with your partner. This helps create a more balanced, soul-level connection.

Communication is a cornerstone of Venus in Gemini. Keep the lines open with your Twin Flame, especially about your needs, desires and any feelings of restlessness. Regularly check in with each other to ensure you're both on the same page and don't hesitate to express what's on your mind. This openness builds trust and emotional safety.

Playfulness and exploration are vital to Venus in Gemini's energy. Keep the fun alive by discovering new things together. Whether it's travelling, trying new hobbies, or simply engaging in lively debates, creating a sense of adventure in your relationship will strengthen the bond and keep both partners engaged.

If you find that the desire for variety sometimes challenges your ability to commit, work on cultivating calm and order in your relationship. This doesn't mean stifling your individuality or the excitement; rather, it involves creating a solid foundation of trust and mutual understanding. A relationship where both partners feel safe can allow for more freedom and growth in the long run.

🌙 Venus in Cancer: Nurturing Love and Emotional Security

This placement brings a natural sensitivity and care for others, especially partners. People with Venus in Cancer are protective and can be incredibly giving, often going to great lengths to ensure their loved ones feel safe and cared for. However, a common challenge for those with Venus in Cancer is the tendency to lose themselves in their relationships. Because they are so attuned to the needs of others, they may neglect their own emotional needs or become overly dependent on their partners for validation and security. The key here is balance. It's important for those with Venus in Cancer to cultivate their own sense of identity, separate from their relationships. Healthy relationships for Venus in Cancer require a foundation of emotional independence – recognizing that both partners are whole individuals with their own needs, desires and boundaries.

In terms of compatibility, Venus in Cancer tends to harmonize well with Venus in Taurus, Cancer and Pisces – signs that share an emotional depth and understanding. However, any relationship can thrive when both partners commit to mutual growth, healthy boundaries and emotional balance.

Self-Help Recommendations for Venus in Cancer

Learn to assert your needs and desires in all areas of life, not just within romantic relationships. This may involve setting boundaries with family, friends and even yourself. Regularly check in with your own feelings and be proactive in expressing your needs, especially when it comes to self-care.

Develop practices that reinforce your emotional independence. Meditation, journalling and connecting with your inner world can help you stay grounded and prevent you from becoming too enmeshed in the emotional lives of others. Don't feel guilty about taking time for yourself.

While it's natural to want to care for others, it's essential to maintain clear boundaries. Reflect on where you might be overextending yourself emotionally and practise saying 'no' when necessary. This will help preserve your energy and sense of self.

People with Venus in Cancer often thrive on emotional closeness, but you should avoid becoming overly dependent on your partner or anyone else for validation. Building self-love and self-compassion is essential for feeling secure in relationships.

Make self-care a priority. As someone who naturally gives a lot to others, it's vital that you regularly replenish your own emotional reserves. Whether through quiet reflection, spending time at home, or engaging in activities that bring you comfort, remember to care for yourself the same way you care for others.

♌ Venus in Leo:
The Heart of the Lion

When Venus is in Leo, love takes centre stage in a grand, passionate and dramatic way. People with this placement crave admiration, respect and unwavering loyalty from their partner. They are generous in love, showering their significant other with attention, affection and extravagant gestures that make their partner feel truly special. In return, they expect the same level of dedication and devotion.

Venus in Leo can spark a powerful and fiery connection, full of intense emotions and electrifying attraction. However, this passion can sometimes lead to clashes of ego or an ongoing need for external validation. The challenge here is to balance the desire for attention and admiration with the need to maintain healthy independence within the relationship.

In relationships, Venus in Leo is most complementary with Venus in Leo itself, Libra and Scorpio. These signs can offer the emotional depth, loyalty and mutual admiration that profoundly resonate with your desires for love.

Self-Help Tips for Venus in Leo

The desire for admiration from others is natural, but make sure to validate and honour yourself before seeking external recognition. Cultivate a strong sense of self-worth that doesn't rely on the approval of others. When you love and appreciate yourself deeply, your relationships will be more balanced and fulfilling.

While your love is all-consuming, it's crucial to remember that your identity doesn't come solely from your relationship. Take time for yourself, pursue your passions and establish your own sense of purpose. This will help prevent any co-dependent tendencies and encourage a healthier, more equal dynamic in your Divine Union.

In the heat of passion, Venus in Leo can sometimes stir up power struggles. To avoid unnecessary conflicts, be aware of moments when your pride or your partner's might get in the way of communication. Strive for humility and understanding, especially in emotionally charged situations. This will allow both partners to express themselves authentically without feeling threatened.

Venus in Leo is ruled by the Sun, which brings out a deep love for creativity and self-expression. Engage in activities that allow you to shine in your own way – whether that's through art, performance, or simply dressing in a way that makes you feel confident and powerful. Expressing yourself freely will help you feel more centred, balanced and whole.

You have a generous heart, and that's a beautiful trait. But remember that love is a two-way street. Be mindful of the need to give and receive love equally. By allowing yourself to receive as much as you give, you'll create a more harmonious and reciprocal connection, not just with your Twin Flame but with everyone you love.

♍ Venus in Virgo:
Love Through Service and Care

With Venus in Virgo, love is expressed through practicality, thoughtfulness and an acute attention to detail. People with this placement show affection by taking care of their partner's needs – whether that's through acts of service, offering support, or ensuring everything runs smoothly. They value reliability and seek a sense of order and stability in relationships, often looking for perfection in their partners and the connection itself.

However, the idealistic drive for perfection can sometimes lead to criticism or an overly analytical approach to love, where the flaws in both their partner and the relationship are magnified. Venus in Virgo can bring healing energy, but also challenges related to self-acceptance, releasing unrealistic expectations and the desire to 'fix' their partner. The key to growth in this placement is learning to acknowledge imperfection, both within themselves and in others.

Venus in Virgo can be highly compatible with Venus in Cancer, Pisces and Virgo. These signs can offer the emotional depth, nurturing energy and understanding that resonate with Venus in Virgo's desire for balance and harmony in relationships.

Self-Help Tips for Venus in Virgo

With Venus in Virgo, there can be a tendency to focus on what's wrong or could be improved. Practise seeing beauty in imperfection, within yourself and in your partner. Acknowledge that no one is perfect, and that that's what makes love so rich and real. Release the need to 'fix' and instead savour each moment for what it is.

People with Venus in Virgo often hold themselves to very high standards. This can lead to feelings of inadequacy or self-criticism. Make a conscious effort to practise self-compassion. Acknowledge your strengths and achievements and let go of the internal pressure to always be perfect. When you are kind to yourself, you'll naturally extend that same compassion to others.

While you love helping and supporting your partner, it's crucial to ensure you're not neglecting your own needs. Learn to strike a balance between offering care and allowing yourself to receive it. Don't forget that others value self-care just as much as service – both in a relationship and in life in general.

Schedule yourself time to recharge and reconnect with your own desires.

Venus in Virgo can lead to a tendency to idealize what a relationship should be and how a partner should behave. It's important to let go of rigid expectations and allow relationships to evolve naturally. Focus on what's real and present, rather than striving for an unattainable ideal. By releasing these expectations, you create more space for genuine connection and acceptance.

Your attention to detail is a gift, but it's easy to get caught up in minutiae and in what's lacking or needs improvement. Make a habit of practising gratitude for the little things – whether it's your partner's thoughtful gesture, a moment of connection, or simply the day-to-day care and love you both share. Rise above sometimes and see the bigger picture. This can help shift your perspective and remind you of the richness of your relationship, even in its imperfections.

♎ Venus in Libra:
The Art of Harmonious Love

As Venus rules Libra, this placement brings a natural affinity for beauty, balance and harmony in relationships. People with Venus in Libra are often drawn to partnerships that feel peaceful, fair and aesthetically pleasing. They are diplomatic by nature, with an intuitive ability to read the needs of others, making them excellent at creating connection and understanding.

Venus in Libra fosters a sense of equality and mutual respect, with a strong desire for companionship and partnership. These individuals thrive when they feel a sense of fairness and unity.

However, the desire to keep the peace and avoid conflict can sometimes lead them to over-compromise or suppress their own feelings, which may prevent deeper emotional growth. To truly flourish in relationships, it's important for those with Venus in Libra to strike a balance between harmony and authentic self-expression.

Venus in Libra resonates well with Venus in Aries, Taurus and Libra. These signs complement Libra's love of balance and beauty, offering a strong foundation for harmony and mutual respect in relationships.

Self-Help Tips for Venus in Libra

While your instinct may be to avoid disagreements or keep the peace, it's essential to understand that conflict can be a catalyst for growth in relationships. Don't shy away from tough conversations; instead, learn to approach them with a spirit of openness and mutual respect. Healthy conflict can strengthen the bond between you and your partner, fostering deeper emotional intimacy.

With Venus in Libra, you may sometimes prioritize your partner's happiness over your own, but it's important to remember that a healthy relationship requires balance. Take time to nurture your own emotional needs and desires, even if doing so feels uncomfortable at first. When you are fulfilled within yourself, you'll bring a more authentic and empowered energy into your relationship. Practise expressing your needs and desires clearly and confidently. Healthy boundaries create a strong foundation for mutual respect, preventing you from losing yourself in the process of keeping the peace.

Venus in Libra thrives on connection but make time to nurture your own sense of self-worth. Spend time in self-reflection and cultivate self-love by recognizing your unique qualities. When you feel grounded in your own identity, your relationships will naturally become more fulfilling and harmonious.

Harmony is a core value for you but remember that balance doesn't always mean compromise. Sometimes it means finding middle ground that respects your needs as well as your partner's. Strive for a relationship dynamic where both partners contribute equally, support each other's growth and celebrate each other's individuality.

♏ Venus in Scorpio:
Love Through Depth and Transformation

Venus in Scorpio brings a love that is intense, passionate and all-consuming. People with this placement crave emotional connections that go beyond the surface. They seek relationships that can transform them, pushing them to confront their deepest desires and fears. For those with Venus in Scorpio, love is rarely ever casual – it's a journey of emotional depth, growth and often healing. However, this intensity can sometimes lead to feelings of jealousy, possessiveness and obsession. People with Venus in Scorpio may find themselves struggling with trust issues or a fear of betrayal, making vulnerability particularly challenging.

Venus in Scorpio can feel in tune with Venus in Leo, Scorpio and Pisces. These signs can offer the emotional depth, passion and transformative potential that resonate deeply with Scorpio's intense approach to love.

Self-Help Tips for Venus in Scorpio

One of the biggest challenges for Venus in Scorpio is allowing oneself to be vulnerable. There may be a fear of getting hurt or betrayed, but true intimacy comes from being open and authentic with your partner. Practise small acts of vulnerability – whether it's sharing your fears or expressing your needs – and trust that these moments of openness will build a richer connection over time.

With Venus in Scorpio, there's often a desire to control the dynamics of a relationship to protect oneself from emotional pain. While it's natural to want security, try to release the need to control every aspect of the connection. Letting go of control allows you to experience love in a more expansive and freeing way.

The transformative power of Venus in Scorpio often involves confronting difficult emotions or past wounds. Take time to reflect on your emotional patterns, especially in relationships and in terms of how much you are projecting yourself on others. Are there recurring fears or insecurities, such as fear of betrayal or abandonment? Healing these aspects by cultivating self-awareness – whether through journalling, therapy, or meditation – will help you approach love with a clearer, more empowered mindset.

Scorpio's intense passion can sometimes manifest as possessiveness. Recognize that while these emotions are valid, they can be limiting if not managed. Work on building trust within yourself and your relationship. Remind yourself that love is about connection, not ownership. When you cultivate trust, you create a healthier, more balanced relationship dynamic.

Venus in Scorpio's intense energy can often lead to a focus on the importance of transforming others, sometimes to the point of unhealthy obsession with that other person, but true transformation starts within. Focus on nurturing your own self-love and emotional wellbeing. Engage in practices that help you reconnect with your sense of self-worth, such as meditation, creative expression, or spending time alone to reflect. When you are whole and centred within yourself, you attract relationships that mirror that wholeness.

♐ Venus in Sagittarius:
Love for Freedom, Adventure and Exploration

With Venus in Sagittarius, love is an adventurous, free-spirited journey. People with this placement are drawn to relationships that are intellectually stimulating, exciting and filled with new experiences. They value their independence and seek partners who share their curiosity, love for knowledge and desire to explore the world – whether through travel, deep philosophical discussions, or embracing new ways of thinking.

In a Twin Flame relationship, Venus in Sagittarius can bring a dynamic, spontaneous connection filled with growth and discovery. However, the desire for freedom and personal space can sometimes lead to restlessness or a reluctance to explore deeper, more emotionally intense conversations. For these relationships to thrive, both partners must respect each other's need for independence while also being willing to confront uncomfortable or difficult topics when necessary. Finding the balance between adventure and emotional depth is key. Venus in Sagittarius is potentially most compatible with Venus in Gemini, Sagittarius and Aquarius.

Self-Help Tips for Venus in Sagittarius

While you thrive on freedom and adventure, it's important to remember that deep emotional connection is just as vital as intellectual and physical exploration. Try to engage in heartfelt conversations with your partner, even if they feel uncomfortable. Vulnerability and openness may not come as naturally to you, but they are essential for long-term intimacy. By embracing emotional depth, you allow your relationship to evolve beyond just fun and adventure.

Your love for freedom is part of what makes you an exciting and dynamic partner. It's essential to honour your need for personal space and time to pursue your own passions. However, be mindful of how you communicate this need to your partner – being clear about your boundaries ensures that your desire for independence doesn't lead to emotional distance or a sense of neglect in the relationship.

While spontaneity and excitement are key to your love life, be careful not to let restlessness or fear of commitment sabotage your deeper connections. You need a partner who understands and appreciates your need for adventure, but also one who can ground you in the stability of a committed, loving partnership.

As a Sagittarius, you're naturally drawn to growth and expansion – whether that's through travel, learning, or new experiences. Incorporate self-reflection into this journey. Regularly take time to assess what you've learned from your relationships and experiences. Ask yourself: 'How have I grown? What areas of myself am I ready to evolve?' This will help ensure that your relationships remain transformative and fulfilling.

Sometimes, Venus in Sagittarius can lead to a tendency to avoid difficult or intense conversations in favour of light-heartedness and fun. To build a healthy relationship, it's essential to communicate openly about your needs, desires and boundaries. Be honest about your need for space at certain times but also make sure to regularly communicate your appreciation for your partner and the importance of the relationship in your life.

♑ Venus in Capricorn: Love Through Commitment and Stability

Venus in Capricorn approaches love with a practical, grounded mindset. People with this placement are often drawn to partners who share their ambition, drive and desire for stability. For them, love is about building a solid foundation that can stand the test of time, and they approach relationships with a sense of responsibility and purpose.

Venus in Capricorn can create a connection that is rooted in trust and security. However, it may also bring challenges around vulnerability and emotional expression. Those with this placement may tend to prioritize practical concerns – like career, stability, or duty – over emotional intimacy, which can create distance in their relationships. There may also be a fear of letting go, causing them to stay in relationships past their expiration date, even when they no longer serve their growth.

Learning to balance practicality with emotional openness is key to maintaining a healthy and fulfilling connection. Venus in Capricorn is perhaps most compatible with Venus in Capricorn itself, or Cancer and Pisces.

Self-Help Tips for Venus in Capricorn

With Venus in Capricorn, there's a strong tendency to prioritize stability and practicality, which can sometimes lead to emotional suppression. Challenge yourself to open up more to your partner, even when it feels uncomfortable. Express your feelings, fears and desires with vulnerability. Emotional connection is just as vital as material stability in a relationship and being open with your partner will deepen the bond between you.

People with Venus in Capricorn often feel a strong sense of duty and commitment to their relationships. While loyalty is admirable, it can lead to staying in situations that no longer serve your happiness or growth. Pay attention to your emotional needs and whether they're being met. It's important to recognize when a relationship has reached its natural conclusion, even if it feels difficult to let go.

Ambition and career goals are essential to you, but learn how to balance your professional life with your personal relationships. Make time for your partner and nurture the emotional side of your relationship. Remember, love and connection require effort, not just practical achievements. Setting aside time to invest in your relationship will help create a more balanced and harmonious life.

Venus in Capricorn can sometimes lead to perfectionism, especially in relationships. You may have high expectations of yourself and your partner, which can create pressure and emotional distance. Practise accepting imperfections in both you and your partner. Love thrives in an environment of acceptance and understanding, not rigid expectations.

Allowing room for mistakes and growth will foster deeper intimacy.

Venus in Capricorn often places the needs of others first, but it's crucial to remember that self-love and self-care are the foundation of any healthy relationship. Take time to care for your own emotional and physical wellbeing. Be patient with yourself, especially when it comes to emotional expression. Over time, as you grow more comfortable with vulnerability and self-compassion, your relationships will naturally become more fulfilling.

♒ Venus in Aquarius: Love for Freedom and Uniqueness

Venus in Aquarius values individuality, independence and unconventional love. People with this placement are often drawn to partners who are intellectually stimulating, unique and openminded. They seek relationships that allow them to retain their sense of freedom and personal identity while exploring deeper, more expansive connections. For Venus in Aquarius, love isn't about adhering to traditional norms – it's about forging a bond that's progressive, authentic and transcendent.

This Venus placement seeks a partner who can challenge them intellectually, inspire them and engage in conversations that push the boundaries of conventional thinking. However, because of their strong drive for independence, there can be a tendency towards emotional detachment or aloofness. Both partners must respect each other's need for personal space while avoiding emotional distance that could prevent deeper intimacy. Venus in Aquarius finds the most compatibility with Venus in Gemini, Sagittarius and Aquarius.

Self-Help Tips for Venus in Aquarius

Venus in Aquarius thrives on intellectual and spiritual connection, but emotional intimacy can sometimes feel challenging. Try to create space for vulnerability, even if it feels uncomfortable. Emotional connection doesn't mean losing your independence – it's about creating a balance where both partners can share and grow without compromising their individual selves.

Due to a natural fear of being let down or becoming emotionally dependent, there's sometimes a tendency to pull away or keep things at arm's length. To build deeper trust, practise being open about your feelings and needs. Let go of the fear that emotional closeness will lead to dependence and instead learn to view intimacy as a strengthening of your unique bond. Trust that a strong connection can enhance both your individuality and your relationship.

While your need for independence is essential, it's also important to strike a balance between freedom and togetherness in a relationship. Schedule time for your own pursuits and passions but also invest time in enriching the emotional and intellectual connection with your partner. A healthy relationship with Venus in Aquarius is one where both partners feel free to be themselves yet are still deeply engaged with one another.

It can be easy for Venus in Aquarius to become emotionally detached, especially when things get too intense or either partner seems vulnerable. Practise remaining emotionally present even when it feels safer to distance yourself. This can be done through small gestures of affection, clear communication, or simply being there for your partner during emotional moments. Emotional availability strengthens the bond, making it more than just an intellectual connection.

One of the most beautiful aspects of Venus in Aquarius is the deep respect for individuality. Continue to celebrate your own uniqueness and that of your partner. Encourage each other's personal growth and be supportive of individual pursuits, but also be intentional about coming together in ways that nurture your shared values and goals. A relationship with Venus in Aquarius thrives when both people are free to explore their own paths while still growing together.

♓ Venus in Pisces:
The Dreamy, Compassionate Lover

People with this Venus placement are drawn to love that feels transcendent, often seeking a connection that goes beyond the physical and enters the realm of the spiritual or emotional. They tend to idealize love, viewing it through rose-coloured glasses, and may envision their ideal relationship as a perfect, 'written in the stars' kind of bond.

Venus in Pisces can create a dreamy, almost otherworldly bond in relationships. However, there can also be a tendency for people with this placement to lose themselves in the relationship, either by neglecting personal boundaries or by avoiding the more difficult, real-world aspects of love. For Venus in Pisces, the key to growth is learning to ground their idealism and navigate the balance between their dream world and practical, healthy emotional boundaries. Venus in Pisces is most compatible with Venus in Scorpio, Capricorn and Pisces.

Self-Help Tips for Venus in Pisces

With Venus in Pisces, it's easy to become lost in the fantasy of love, idealizing a partner or the relationship itself. While it's beautiful to love dream, it's important to also stay grounded. Regularly assess whether your expectations of love and your partner are realistic and take time to check in with yourself. Be aware of any tendencies to over-romanticize or escape difficult emotions, and challenge yourself to appreciate love in its full, imperfect glory.

The compassionate and selfless nature of Venus in Pisces can sometimes lead to you putting the needs of others above your own, often to your own detriment. Learn to establish and respect healthy boundaries in relationships. Make sure you take time to nurture yourself, emotionally and physically, without feeling guilty. Boundaries don't diminish love; they create space for mutual respect, personal growth and lasting emotional connection.

Avoidance of uncomfortable emotions can be a tendency for Venus in Pisces, especially when the reality of a relationship feels less than ideal. However, growth in love comes from facing difficult emotions head-on, whether they relate to conflict, fear of rejection, or past wounds. Allow yourself the emotional space to experience these feelings and trust that confronting them will lead to healing and a stronger, more authentic connection.

In your quest for unity with your partner, it's easy to lose sight of your own identity. Spend time exploring your own passions, interests and goals outside of the relationship. When you feel whole and fulfilled on your own, you're able to give and receive love in a more balanced way. Remember, healthy relationships are built by individuals who are complete within themselves.

Venus in Pisces can sometimes attract relationships that seem ideal on the surface but may be unhealthy or unsustainable. Trust your intuition but also practise discernment. Reflect on whether the relationship is genuinely nourishing your spirit or is based on a fantasy or need for escapism. Let your heightened intuition guide you towards relationships that support your growth and wellbeing, while letting go of those that don't align with your highest good.

The Heart of the Matter

Your Venus sign can reveal a lot about how you give and receive love. It's not just about attraction – Venus represents your deepest needs in relationships. Understanding the position of Venus in your birth chart can empower you on your Twin Flame Journey; if you are already in a relationship, then recognizing the placement of both partners' Venus signs and the areas of compatibility between them can help your connection flourish. Venus reveals where your hearts can align and where potential challenges may arise, giving you the opportunity to grow, heal and strengthen your bond.

Don't despair if you read the above descriptions and discover that your partner's Venus sign isn't among those likely to be compatible with your own; if there is a desire between two people to make a relationship work, then even the most incompatible Venus signs can learn and grow together. Indeed, there is wisdom in the idea that opposites attract – and sometimes relationships that appear to be completely wrong at surface level can end up being completely right. There are no fixed rules in astrology or in love, just guidelines and the whispers of your heart.

Notice and support the qualities of your Venus sign and have faith that every step you take – whether by yourself or in a relationship – brings you closer to experiencing the divine love at the core of your Twin Flame Path.

Brave Your Elements

One of the most illuminating tools for understanding the dynamics of Twin Flame relationships is the study of the four elements: fire, water, earth and air. Each element carries its own elemental energy, influencing your emotional needs and desires in a romantic union.

By exploring the elemental nature of Venus signs, we can begin to see the underlying emotional and psychological patterns in our romantic connections. What follows is a closer look at each element and the insights it offers when viewed through the lens of Venus. Understanding and discussing these elemental influences can help partners navigate challenges more consciously and harmoniously. It also allows individuals to recognize their own strengths and vulnerabilities within the relationship, which can create deeper empathy, growth and alignment on the Twin Flame Journey.

Fire

Venus in fire signs (Aries, Leo, Sagittarius). If your Venus is in a fire sign, you thrive on excitement, passion and freedom in your relationships. You need space to be yourself, to explore and to follow your own path, even within the context of a committed partnership. While you're capable of commitment, what truly ignites your heart is a partner who can match your energy with enthusiasm, spontaneity and bold gestures of affection. You love the thrill of romantic adventure; and feeling free to pursue your dreams, both within and outside of the relationship, is essential to your sense of love and fulfilment.

Earth

Venus in Earth signs (Taurus, Virgo, Capricorn). If your Venus is in one of the earth signs, your emotional wellbeing in a relationship depends heavily on feeling stable, secure and grounded. You crave tangible proof of love – whether that's in the form of consistent actions or reliability, or material expressions like gifts and thoughtful gestures. While you're open to having fun and dreaming with your partner, your heart truly flourishes when there's a sense of permanence and trust. This means you're likely to appreciate practical support, commitment and a relationship that feels reliable, steady and rooted.

Air

Venus in air signs (Gemini, Libra, Aquarius). For Venus in air signs, communication is key to feeling loved and connected. You need mental stimulation and engaging conversations with your partner – sharing ideas, discussing emotions and working through challenges together by means of open dialogue. While you value your independence and need time to yourself, nothing brings you closer to your partner than meaningful exchanges that allow you to explore each other's thoughts and feelings. You're drawn to relationships that encourage intellectual growth and where both partners can articulate their needs, desires and boundaries openly and honestly.

Water

Venus in water signs (Cancer, Scorpio, Pisces). For those with Venus in a water sign, emotional depth and connection are paramount to feeling loved. You need your partner to be highly empathetic and sensitive to your feelings and able to intuitively understand your moods and needs. While there's still room for planning and organizing, what really nurtures your heart is spontaneous, heartfelt expressions of affection – surprises, emotional intimacy and a deep bond that goes beyond the surface. A relationship that feels emotionally safe, where both partners can freely express their vulnerabilities, will resonate most strongly with you.

☊ Your North Node

Your Venus sign is perhaps the most significant indicator in Twin Flame astrology, but it is also worth paying attention to what your reading tells you about your North Node.

The South and North Nodes in your birth chart are not planets or stars but simply astrological calculations related to the positioning of the moon. This isn't the book to explore astrological complexities in depth, but many other resources are available if you want to know more. For the purposes of your Twin Flame Path, the South Node in your chart matters because it suggests your personal karma or personal life lessons to learn. But it is the North Node that points to your potential destiny or the kind of relationship you should be moving towards or looking forward to for your greatest happiness and to nurture your best or highest self. This relationship destiny is something you need to learn to choose or attract; and it can arrive only after you have learned your life lessons.

The North Node in astrology is often referred to as the 'Dragon's Head' and is considered a point of purpose, guiding you towards your highest destiny – and the relationship you have with yourself and with others will tie in with that destiny. The North Node indicates where you are headed, while the South Node represents the patterns, habits and gifts you need to master before you can move forwards. In Divine Unions, the North Node can act as your Twin Flame Path blueprint, offering insight into how you can transcend old Karmic cycles and align with your divine purpose. And when Twin Flames unite, their North Node placements can be particularly significant. By understanding and working with the energies of their North

Nodes, Spiritual Mirrors can achieve not just personal growth, but also a mutual spiritual evolution.

In Twin Flame astrology, the North Node points to what needs to be developed, learned and integrated. Understanding each partner's North Node placement can illuminate the spiritual lessons and challenges that will arise and empower both partners to better understand and support each other on the path to their soul's purpose. For instance, if one Twin's North Node is in Aries and the other's North Node is in Libra, their union may push them towards balancing independence and honesty with partnership and tact. This dynamic may help them learn how to assert themselves while also considering the needs of others, ultimately leading them both towards greater personal and relational harmony.

Here is an overview of the North Node positioning across the zodiac and the relationship destiny it nudges you towards. Remember, this applies to the relationship you have with yourself too. If you are in a relationship you may want to pull up your partner's birth chart alongside yours right now to see if they share the same North or South Node sign or element, or whether your Nodes complement or challenge each other.

North Node in the 12 Signs: An Overview

♈ North Node in Aries

Your Twin Flame Awakening is one of independence, courage and self-assertion. You are learning to step into your power, take risks and prioritize your own desires. This placement encourages you to nurture your individuality and maintain a strong sense of self within your relationships.

○ North Node in Taurus

This Twin Flame placement calls for stability, groundedness and the cultivation of inner peace. Your soul's growth is clustered around material security and developing a deeper connection to the physical world. It encourages you to create a solid foundation, both emotionally and materially, in your relationships and daily life.

♊ North Node in Gemini

The focus here is on communication, curiosity and empathy. You must learn to expand your mind, accept change and go with the flow. This Tv ♋Flame placement is all about intellectual growth, openminded dialogue and emotional regulation, regardless of whether you are in a relationship.

♋ North Node in Cancer

Your Twin Flame Path is centred on nurturing, emotional intelligence and creating a sense of home. You must learn to acknowledge your vulnerability and connect with others authentically. This placement calls for deep emotional bonding and the creation of a loving, supportive environment where you and your partner both feel safe to grow.

North Node in Leo

This placement guides you towards self-expression, creativity and leadership. You must cherish your individuality and learn to be assertive, and comfortable in the spotlight. Your Divine Union elevates whenever you feel creative, playful and passionate.

♍ North Node in Virgo

Your Twin Flame Pilgrimage places a high value on order, precision and service. This placement encourages you to work towards a grounded and disciplined life and to commit fully to self-improvement and to helping others learn and grow alongside you.

♎ North Node in Libra

Balance, harmony, compromise and mutual understanding are key here. Your Twin Flame Journey is all about learning how to navigate life and relationships with fairness, diplomacy and compassion.

♏ North Node in Scorpio

A deep dive into transformation, intimacy and the mystery of life is required. Your Twin Flame Odyssey involves letting go of superficiality and embracing the very real possibility of emotional connection with yourself and others – and awakening spiritually in the process.

♐ North Node in Sagittarius

Your Twin Flame Adventure focuses on expansion, exploration and the quest for higher knowledge. You are meant to seek out adventure, push boundaries, explore the world both physically and spiritually in your search for answers and to live and love with optimism.

♑ North Node in Capricorn

This Twin Flame Journey points you towards ambition, shared responsibility and dedication. You must create lasting structures and take steady, practical steps towards your long-term goals in both your life and your relationships.

♒ North Node in Aquarius

This path leads you towards embracing individuality, innovation and humanitarian ideals. You must think outside the box, connect with likeminded individuals and contribute to the collective while at the same time honouring your own uniqueness.

♓ North Node in Pisces

Yours is a Twin Flame Evolution of spiritual growth, compassion and intuition. Your path in life and in your relationships involves embracing the mystical, tuning into your intuition and connecting with a higher consciousness.

Your Rising Sign

Alongside your Venus and North Node, there is one other placement in Twin Flame astrology you may want to reflect on: your rising sign, also known as your ascendant.

Your rising sign plays a critical role in shaping your outward personality and behaviour and how you present yourself to the world. It represents the 'mask' you wear, the energy or persona you project when others meet you and often how others perceive you. For Twin Flame astrology, the rising sign is worth paying attention to because it is the lens through which both individuals first encounter each other, shaping the initial stages of the relationship and setting the tone for how they might navigate their journey together.

While the sun sign represents your core or essence, the rising sign reveals the qualities you tend to exhibit in public and how you instinctively react to new situations and encounters – which are especially important for Twin Flame astrology. Additionally, because it is your 'mask' rather than your true essence, it is where you can immediately start to make positive adjustments.

The rising sign is often what you notice first when you meet someone and what they first sense intuitively about you. It's the energy that attracts or repels, the first impressions that are made. In a Twin Flame relationship, this placement reveals how each partner will interact with one another on a day-to-day basis. It's their default setting and how they present themselves to the outside world. For example, if your rising sign is a fire sign (Aries, Leo, or Sagittarius), you might immediately give others the impression that you are spontaneous and action-oriented, while an earth rising sing (Taurus, Virgo, or Capricorn) may bring a more grounded, practical presence.

First Impressions

By understanding your ascendant placement, you can deeply comprehend your instinctive approach to life and how others tend to perceive you. First impressions count – although, as we all know from reading *Pride and Prejudice*, they can in time be proved wrong.

In Twin Flame relationships, when two people understand and learn to honour each other's rising signs, and adjust their approach to meet each other's needs, they create a more harmonious dynamic that fosters not just individual growth but also a more intense spiritual connection. The rising sign helps illuminate the path towards unity, where both individuals can shine as their authentic selves while supporting the other in their evolution towards greater love, truth and light.

Here's an overview of the first impression you are likely to make on others, how you initially approach your relationship with yourself or relate to your own inner world.

♈ Aries Rising

With an Aries ascendant, the approach to life is bold, assertive and energetic. People with Aries rising often have a quick, direct approach to challenges and tend to charge into new experiences and relationships headfirst. In a Divine Union, this energy can spark excitement and action but also create a sense of impatience or impulsivity. The challenge is to temper this instinctive drive with greater reflection and consideration for the emotional needs of others.

♉ Taurus Rising

Taurus ascendants tend to present themselves as stable, grounded and sensual. They approach life with a calm, steady pace, seeking comfort, security and beauty in their surroundings. In a Divine Union, this individual brings a sense of peace and consistency. Their challenge may be learning to embrace change and emotional vulnerability, which can feel unsettling to their naturally steady disposition.

♊ Gemini Rising

Gemini ascendants are curious, adaptable, flirty and communicative. They present a lively, sociable exterior and thrive in intellectual exchanges and where there is variety. In

Cosmic Love, this energy creates a dynamic where both partners can explore new ideas and experiences together. However, the challenge for people with Gemini rising is to ground their thoughts and avoid superficiality.

♋ Cancer Rising

Those with Cancer ascendant often come across as nurturing, protective and emotionally attuned to their surroundings. They value emotional security and can be highly intuitive. In Twin Flame relationships, Cancer rising may bring warmth and a deep emotional connection, but the challenge for people with this placement is to move beyond insecurity and trust that love can be unconditional without clinging or overprotecting.

♌ Leo Rising

Leo ascendants exude charisma, creativity and confidence. They tend to have a magnetic personality and often seek to be recognized or admired for their unique qualities. In a Divine Union, a partner with Leo rising can have energy that brings joy, warmth and playfulness, but they may also struggle with their desire for attention or validation. Their challenge is to find balance between self-expression and the needs of their partner and ensure that their love is not driven by ego.

♍ Virgo Rising

Virgo ascendants present themselves as practical, organized and detail-oriented. They often have a methodical approach to life and take pride in helping others and improving situations. In Twin Flame relationships, Virgo rising's energy can create a sense of stability and mutual support, but their challenge is to let go of perfectionism and the tendency to over-analyse, learning to value imperfection and emotional vulnerability.

♎ Libra Rising

Libra ascendants have a natural charm and grace and a strong desire for balance and harmony in their lives. They excel in relationships and often strive to create beauty and peace. In Divine Unions, partners with Libra rising can bring diplomacy, balance and a sense of fairness. Their challenge lies in learning to assert themselves and not always seek external validation but instead to cultivate their own internal peace and confidence.

♏ Scorpio Rising

Scorpio ascendants often present themselves with intensity, mystery and depth. They have a keen ability to perceive underlying truths and aren't afraid of facing life's darker aspects. In Twin Flame relationships, a person with Scorpio rising creates a fierce emotional bond, but their challenge is to release control and jealousy and learn how to trust their partner fully. Their journey involves embracing vulnerability and learning to surrender to love without fear.

♐ Sagittarius Rising

With Sagittarius ascendant, life is seen as an adventure. These people are optimistic and free-spirited and love exploring new horizons. People with Sagittarius rising value independence and freedom. In Divine Unions, they bring excitement, exploration and a broadminded perspective. Their challenge is to commit more fully to the relationship and to ground their expansive energy, learning to balance freedom with practicality and responsibility.

♑ Capricorn Rising

Capricorn ascendants tend to appear reserved, disciplined and ambitious. They approach life with practicality and a strong desire to achieve their goals. In Cosmic Love, Capricorn rising offers a steady, reliable presence, but their challenge is to soften their exterior and welcome in emotional warmth and fun. They must learn to balance their drive for material success with nurturing their relationships.

♒ Aquarius Rising

Aquarius ascendants present themselves as unique, progressive and sometimes eccentric. They are future-oriented and value individuality and social progress. In a Divine Union, a person with Aquarius rising brings innovation, creativity and a desire to break free from societal norms. The challenge for them is connecting on a deeper emotional level with their partner, as their intellectual detachment can sometimes create distance.

♓ Pisces Rising

Pisces ascendants have an ethereal and compassionate energy. Intuitive, empathetic and naturally drawn to the spiritual or artistic realms. In Twin Flame relationships, Pisces rising brings emotional depth, imagination and spiritual insight. The challenge for people with this placement lies in maintaining clear boundaries and not losing themselves in the relationship, learning to ground their dreams into reality.

Beyond Astrology

While astrology can offer unique insight into the dynamics of Cosmic Love, it is by no means the only system of divination that can guide and inform you on your Twin Flame Awakening of self-discovery and spiritual growth. There are many other spiritual and metaphysical tools that can help you understand your personality and the deeper layers of your relationship with your Spiritual Mirror. These systems – each unique in their approach – offer a different lens through which you can explore the nuances of your soul's path and the way you interact with others, particularly in love and relationships.

In this section, we'll explore several powerful divination systems, each of which can increase your understanding of yourself, your love language and your Divine Union.

The Tarot: Unveiling the Inner Self and Relationship Dynamics

The tarot is an ancient system of divination that uses a deck of 78 archetypal cards to explore the energy surrounding a situation or a person. Each card in the tarot represents different aspects of life, from emotional challenges to spiritual lessons, and provides a mirror for the subconscious mind. In a Twin Flame Journey, tarot readings can help illuminate the hidden layers of the relationship, offer guidance on how to navigate conflicts and highlight the spiritual lessons each Twin Flame must learn.

When it comes to Divine Union tarot readings, here are some cards to look out for:

The World and the Fool. These can be particularly revealing when they appear in a spread, as they speak to the power of choice and the search for connection on your Twin Flame Journey.

The Sun. This card speaks to the spontaneous, passionate child within each of us, who seeks warmth and affirmation through connection with their Twin Flame.

The Chariot. This card highlights the balancing of masculine and feminine energies, echoing the yin-yang of the Divine Union dynamic.

The Lovers and the Two of Cups. These cards are perhaps the most significant for the union between Twin Flames because they signify the energy of deeply intense relationships.

Other cards strongly associated with the Twin Flame Path include: the Empress, the High Priestess, the Moon, the Star, the Ace of Cups and the King and Queen of Cups. However, because tarot is dependent on your own intuition, every card in the pack can offer its own profound commentary in a Twin Flame tarot reading.

Tarot-card readings can also shed light on each person's individual growth path – emphasizing the importance of self-love, emotional healing and the need to develop your own sense of wholeness before you can fully merge with another person in love.

THE FOOL.

THE LOVERS.

THE CHARIOT.

THE SUN.

THE WORLD.

Practical Use

A Twin Flame relationship reading can reveal the emotional blocks each partner might face. If you are doing a reading by yourself, my advice would be to start with the archetypal images of the Rider-Waite Tarot Deck and to learn about that deck and the meanings of each card first. One highly recommended and evergreen tarot interpretation read is Rachel Pollack's *Seventy-Eight Degrees of Wisdom*.

Tarot spreads focused on 'how you see each other' or 'what needs healing' can help illuminate both the internal and external challenges each partner is facing.

Pulling specific cards at random to ask about your love language or relationship dynamics or what lies ahead for your heart can help uncover areas of opportunity, miscommunication or misunderstanding.

Choose one card from the following three: the Lovers, the Two of Cups, or the Sun. Use it as your meditation focus for two to five minutes. See what brainstorming associations it brings you.

Numerology: Decoding the Divine Blueprint

Numerology is the age-old study of the energetic influence of numbers on our lives. Each number has its own vibration and energy and numerology is a way of interpreting hidden patterns of numbers in your life and what they mean for your history, personality, relationships and even the timing of significant events. Your Life Path number offers insight into your soul's purpose in this lifetime (this number is calculated by adding together all the digits in your birth date), while your Expression number reveals your natural talents, challenges and potential (this is calculated using your full birth name, with each letter of the alphabet assigned a number from 1 to 9 in sequence – you start with A = 1 and when you hit 9 you return to 1, and so on).

In Divine Unions, numerology can be an invaluable tool to understand the deep connection between you and your partner. The numbers in your birth chart will highlight not only the way you express yourself but also the patterns and lessons your soul is working through in the relationship. For example, a Twin Flame couple may share a significant Life Path number, suggesting they have come together to work through similar life lessons.

Practical Use

Use numerology to identify your Life Path and Expression numbers to gain a richer understanding of your core desires and purpose. Do some of your own research first so you know more about numerology and how to interpret the numbers.

Consider the 'compatibility' of Life Path numbers between Twin Flames. Often, complementary numbers suggest a harmonious dynamic, while challenging numbers can reveal the areas that need healing in the relationship.

As explored on page 117, pay attention to recurring number sequences (like 11:11) as these may be messages from your higher self or guides about the Divine Union. Repeating 1s are often thought to be a Master Number sign that you have encountered your Twin Flame. Repeating 2s can indicate that lessons are being learned. Repeating 3s suggest self-empowerment and 8s infinity and beyond.

Human Design:
Discovering Your Unique Energy Blueprint

Human Design is a relatively new system that blends elements of astrology, the *I Ching* (see page 193), the Kabbalah Tree of Life and the chakra system to provide a highly detailed map of your personality, strengths, weaknesses and the way you interact with the world. This system identifies your unique energy type (there are five types: Manifestor, Generator, Manifesting Generator, Projector and Reflector) and helps you understand how you make decisions, how you interact with others and how you can live in alignment with your true self.

For Twin Flames, Human Design can offer helpful insight into how each partner's energy interacts. This system shows where there is synergy and where there might be tension, making it easier for you and your Spiritual Mirror to honour each other's energetic needs and learn to coexist in a way that supports each other's growth.

Practical Use

Discover your Human Design type and strategy (the optimal way to make decisions) to understand how you should approach decision-making within the relationship.

Learn about your authority (your inner decision-making system) and how you can support your Twin Flame by allowing them to follow their own authority.

Examine your centres (energy hubs) and how they align with or challenge your partner's centres, offering guidance on how to best complement one another's energy.

A word of caution: there are Human Design chart generators online but, unlike astrology, because the system is complex, you will often need a Human Design coach to help you interpret them and these coaches and courses can be expensive.

The Enneagram:
Understanding Your Core Motivation

The Enneagram is a powerful personality system that categorizes individuals into nine core types, each defined by a basic fear and a basic desire. This system offers deep psychological insights and reveals how we view the world, how we react to stress and how we approach relationships. Understanding your Enneagram type can help you and your Twin Flame understand each other's core motivations, triggers and patterns of behaviour.

The Enneagram can uncover unconscious behaviours that may lead to conflict within Cosmic Love, as well as strengths that can support growth. For example, a Type One (the Perfectionist) may have a strong inner critic that affects their ability to express love freely, while a Type Nine (the Peacemaker) might avoid conflict, leading to misunderstandings. Through Enneagram awareness, Twin Flames can develop empathy for each other and work through challenges in a healthy, constructive way.

Practical Use

Take time to learn about the Enneagram system and how to use it to benefit your personal growth. Then use it to identify your Twin Flame's type, which will shed light on your core fears and desires.

Understand the relationship dynamics between certain types. For example, a Type Three (the Achiever) may struggle to connect emotionally with a Type Four (the Individualist), but when both types understand their differences they can create deeper emotional intimacy.

Practise using the growth arrows in the Enneagram system, which show you the direction of growth for each type. Understanding where you and your Spiritual Mirror are evolving can foster greater support and understanding.

The Akashic Records: Twin Flames Reading

The Akashic Records are believed to be a metaphysical imprint of all souls' past, present and future experiences, holding the collective wisdom of the universe. A reading of the Akashic Records involves accessing this ethereal database through meditation and visualization to gain insights into your personal life paths, purpose and spiritual growth. Doing a reading can help individuals better understand their life's challenges, uncover hidden potential and guide them towards alignment with their higher self, their Twin Flame and soul's purpose. Think of your Akashic Record as an energetic imprint of the state of your soul based on your current mindset. It can reveal areas of potential growth and conflict.

To open, read and close the Akashic Records for a Twin Flame reading, you can follow this step-by-step process:

Find a quiet, comfortable space where you can safely be alone and can focus without distractions. Take a few deep breaths, ground yourself and clear your mind of any lingering thoughts.

Clearly state your intention for the reading, such as:

'I [say your full legal name] ask to access the Akashic Records to gain insight into my connection with my Twin Flame and understand our souls' journey together. I ask that all information be for the highest good of all involved.'

You may also ask specific questions, such as:

'What is the current state of my Divine Union?'
'What blockages exist between me and my Twin Flame?'

Once you've opened the records, trust the information you receive. This may come in the form of thoughts, feelings, images, or intuitive impressions. Pay attention to any subtle shifts in energy or sensations within your body. As you receive answers, take note of recurring themes, symbols, or messages that seem relevant to your relationship with your Twin Flame. These insights can often give clarity on patterns, soul contracts, or life lessons tied to your union.

The Akashic Records may reveal more than just a connection with your Spiritual Mirror – they could show Karmic cycles, past-life connections, or spiritual guidance that helps you better understand your relationship dynamics.

When you're ready to conclude the reading, express your gratitude to the Akashic Records, your guides and your higher self for the insight received. Use a closing statement or prayer to respectfully close the records, such as:

> 'I [use your full legal name] now close the Akashic Records with gratitude and trust that all the wisdom shared today will serve my highest good. I thank you for your guidance and protection.'

Take a few moments to breathe deeply and come back to the present moment. You might feel a sense of release or completion. Drink some water or perform a grounding technique to integrate the experience fully. After your session, reflect on the messages received. Journalling or meditating on the insights can help enrich your understanding and allow you to integrate the guidance into your daily life.

Remember, Akashic Records readings are personal and intuitive, so each experience can vary. Trust the process and the wisdom that unfolds during your Twin Flame reading.

Note: Akashic Record work is a lifestyle in the same way that walking the Twin Flame Path is. If you want to take a deeper look at the state of your soul, the rewards can be great and you might want to seek out my book *The Akashic Records*.

The *I Ching*: Embracing the Wisdom of Change

The *I Ching*, also known as the *Book of Changes*, is an Ancient Chinese divination system that uses 64 hexagrams to represent the flow of energy in the universe. Each hexagram provides guidance on how to move through life's transitions with grace and balance. In the context of Twin Flames, the *I Ching* offers guidance on how to approach the inevitable changes and challenges in a relationship, helping both partners find equilibrium amid transformation.

The *I Ching* speaks to the flow of energies between the masculine and feminine and the ebb and flow of personal development, and shows how to align with the greater forces at work in your life. For Twin Flames, the *I Ching* can help you understand when to act, when to step back and when to surrender to the natural cycles of life and love.

Practical Use

Make time to learn as much as you can about the *I Ching* before doing a reading. Then use the *I Ching* to ask specific questions about your relationship and receive insight into the energies at play.

When facing conflict, the *I Ching* can offer wisdom on the timing of actions, revealing whether it is the right moment to take bold steps or whether you should allow things to unfold naturally.

Reflect on the hexagrams that appear in your readings and their relevance to the current phase of your Twin Flame Journey, allowing the teachings of the *I Ching* to guide you through periods of uncertainty or transition.

Twin Flame Crystal Companions

Crystals are powerful tools for energy alignment; and when it comes to attracting your Twin Flame, they can be particularly effective in helping you tap into both self-love and harmonious relationships. The essence of Divine Union is balance and unity and crystals can facilitate this by clearing blockages, elevating your vibration and creating space for deeper connection with yourself and with others. Working with crystals involves wearing or carrying them with you, placing them in your home or workplace and using them as a focal point in meditations.

Practical Use

For self-love. Before you can attract your Twin Flame, it's crucial to cultivate a profound sense of self-love and self-worth. Crystals like rose quartz, amethyst and rhodonite are excellent allies in this process. These stones resonate with the heart chakra and help heal emotional wounds, release negative self-beliefs and enhance feelings of self-compassion and self-acceptance. By meditating with these crystals or simply placing them near you, you can strengthen your connection to your own heart and encourage love, kindness and forgiveness to flow freely from within. This self-love is essential because only by loving yourself can you fully attract and accept the love of your Twin Flame.

For healing your heart. Divine Unions are transformative, often requiring deep healing of past wounds – both individual and collective. Crystals like black tourmaline and smoky quartz can help clear negative energy and protect your aura, while clear quartz amplifies your intention to heal and grow. These stones assist in breaking down emotional barriers and release any toxic energies that may be preventing you from stepping into the fullness of who you are meant to be. When these blockages are cleared, you create more space for the kind of loving relationship that Twin Flames offer.

For energetic balance. When you are in alignment with your higher self, the universe works to bring you closer to your Twin Flame. Crystals like citrine, carnelian and sunstone work with your solar-plexus chakra to boost confidence, clarity and personal power. By working with these stones, you can increase your ability to attract positive opportunities and experiences, including a harmonious Divine Union. These crystals help to bring balance to your own energy, which in turn will magnetize a Twin Flame who mirrors that energy back to you.

For intuition. Attracting your Twin Flame is not just about external action – it's also about trusting your intuition and being open to signs and synchronicities. Crystals like labradorite, sodalite and moonstone can enhance your psychic abilities and intuition, allowing you to better understand your inner guidance. These stones help you recognize when the universe is nudging you towards a potential connection and can deepen your awareness of your own spiritual journey.

For harmonizing relationships. Once you're on the path towards your Twin Flame, maintaining balance and harmony within the relationship becomes essential. Crystals like amethyst, lapis lazuli and rhodochrosite can support emotional clarity and open communication, helping to keep both partners grounded and heart-centred. These crystals also encourage mutual respect and understanding, ensuring that the relationship remains healthy, nurturing and spiritually fulfilling.

In conclusion, crystals can support your journey towards attracting your Spiritual Mirror by fostering self-love, healing past wounds, aligning your energies, enhancing intuition and nurturing a balanced relationship. Working with crystals can be a powerful way to open the door to divine love and prepare your heart and soul to receive your Twin Flame when the time is right.

A Tapestry of Love Wisdom

While astrology is an incredibly powerful tool for understanding the dynamics of Cosmic Love, the other divination systems outlined here can also offer you additional layers of insight and clarity. You can gain a more comprehensive understanding of your Twin Flame Pilgrimage by exploring any of these systems.

You may want to specialize in one system or work with several of them simultaneously. Each one offers a unique perspective and when their insights are combined, they create a rich tapestry of wisdom that can guide you towards greater self-awareness, increased empathy for others and a more harmonious relationship if that is your goal. Ultimately, the key to any Twin Flame Path is love – both self-love and the love you share with your counterpart and others. Using these illuminating self-help tools daily can help you navigate the twists and turns of your journey with greater ease, trust, alignment and a touch of magic.

To allow divination systems like astrology to support you on your Twin Flame Odyssey is to admit that there exist forces greater than you and that you are not alone. These time-honoured systems can be especially educational, comforting and therapeutic when your heart is broken or when you feel lost, unsupported and lonely. They can help you appreciate that each time you feel you are messing up, or like giving up on love, is an opportunity to go even deeper within. A chance to understand that you are never getting things wrong, just making decisions from your current point of personal and spiritual growth. You are simply doing what you need to do and living your meaning and purpose, which is to experience all the highs and lows on your Twin Flame Journey and in the process find your right love direction.

In this light, there are no relationship mistakes, only lessons to get you to where you are destined to be, which is back to yourself and your unconditionally loving soul. And getting right to the heart of your soul is the theme of the next chapter. Don't hesitate now. You are already on your Twin Flame Adventure, remember. Just keep living fully, learning deeply and loving on.

5

DREAMWORK AND THE TWIN FLAME JOURNEY

There is a natural and instantly accessible way to help you understand exactly where you are on your Twin Flame Path and therefore make better relationship decisions. A way to see the current state of your inside-out relationship clearly reflected in the decisions you make about your life and your interactions with others. It's a seriously neglected personal- and spiritual-growth tool that gets right to the heart of the matter and it reveals itself to you every single night. This is the topsy-turvy world of your nocturnal dreams.

I Met You in a Dream!

We all have dreams. Some are vivid, others are fleeting, but all of them have the potential to guide us in our personal, emotional and spiritual journeys. For those on the Twin Flame Path, dream interpretation can take on an even deeper significance. Dreams offer glimpses into the soul connection that awaits or has already begun. Even before you meet your Spiritual Mirror in the physical world, your dreams can begin to show you the energy of the bond you share. They are windows into the mysteries of your soul's journey and they hold powerful messages, both personal and universal.

You may find that your dreams become more vivid, realistic, intense and even precognitive before you meet your Twin Flame.

As you progress through the Twin Flame Journey, your dreams can act as your sacred guides. They can help you navigate through challenges, offer insight into your emotional landscape and give you a glimpse of the spiritual work ahead. In this chapter, we'll explore how dreamwork serves as a powerful tool for understanding yourself better, navigating your relationships and attracting or nurturing your Divine Union. You'll also learn how to interpret your dreams, as well as practical exercises to enhance your dreamwork and spiritual growth.

Dreams as a Portal to Twin Flame Recognition

Before meeting your Twin Flame in physical reality, the soul connection you share often reveals itself through dreams. These dreams can range from symbolic and abstract to highly vivid and emotional, occasionally literal, but all of them serve as a precursor to the deep spiritual reunion that awaits. Your soul, and possibly even your Spiritual Mirror's soul, may communicate through the dream world long before you meet in the physical realm.

These dreams might not always appear clear or direct, and they might even present themselves in enigmatic, symbolic or sometimes disorienting forms. The emotions tied to these dreams, however, are often unmistakable. You may wake up feeling inexplicably elated, peaceful, or even overwhelmed. The sense of recognition is strong, even if you can't fully articulate why. This powerful connection you experience in the dream world is a preview of the intense, magnetic bond that will manifest once the two of you physically unite. Some people even report hugging their Twin Flame in a dream and being told to trust the universe as they are on their way.

The most common signs of Cosmic Love dreams – whether before or after meeting them in real life – tend to reflect key themes of recognition, intense emotional connection, lovemaking and spiritual union. These dreams offer symbolic glimpses into the future, helping you prepare for whatever potentials lie ahead.

Common Twin Flame Dream Signs

Your Twin Flame can manifest in your dreams in various ways even before you meet. Some people experience intense dreams of union, while others may see glimpses of their Spiritual Mirror in symbolic or metaphysical forms. The uniting factor with these dreams is that they usually carry an emotional or spiritual charge that resonates long after waking.

Symbolic familiarity. A common experience for many Twin Flames is the sensation of meeting someone in their dreams who feels incredibly familiar, even though you've never seen or met them before in the physical world. There's a feeling of recognition with a dream stranger that goes beyond mere appearance – it's as if you are reuniting with an old friend or partner, someone you've known for lifetimes.

In these dreams, the sense of peace, comfort and familiarity may overwhelm you while the setting may be entirely *un*familiar. This contrast can be disorienting yet comforting. You might even see your Spiritual Mirror in an altered form, such as through an animal or in abstract imagery, but the energy and emotional connection are so strong that there's no doubt in your mind that you've met your twin.

Union dreams. Twin Flame dreams of union can be remarkably healing. You might find yourself not just sensing or knowing your Twin Flame is near but sharing a quiet loving moment too – holding hands, talking to each other or gazing into each other's eyes. Whether the other person is your partner or a stranger you have yet to meet, these union dreams often bring with them an overwhelming sense of love, contentment and fulfilment. There may be moments of clarity or powerful emotional release that leaves you feeling deeply satisfied, as though you've come home to yourself. These moments of blissful union in your dreams prepare your heart for the eventual real-world reunion, whether that happens through a new relationship or through spiritual awakening, guiding you to a space where you can experience true unity and unconditional love.

Recurrent dreams of separation and struggle. Dreams of union are beautiful and comforting, but the Twin Flame Odyssey often involves struggles and periods of separation that can be reflected or foreshadowed in your dreams. These dreams are an essential part of the healing process, as they help you face fears and emotional wounds that must be addressed for the union to be successful. Dreams of conflict or disconnection reflect internal struggles, past hurts, or limiting beliefs that are preventing you from fully embracing your Divine Union. If you experience dreams of arguments, separations, or confusion with people you know or don't know, these may be reflections of emotional imbalances or unresolved issues either within yourself or in your past relationships. These dreams are often invitations to explore your shadow self and work through the unresolved emotions that stand between you and your Twin Flame's reunion. The more you acknowledge and process these emotions, the more they can shift towards healing and integration.

Dreams of making love. You may wake up with a steamy dream on your mind and your dream affair was either with someone you know or with a stranger. If you know this dream lover in real life, it is natural to wonder whether you are attracted to them. This is often not the case, however. Instead, they represent an aspect of your personality that you need to get more intimate with. If your dream lover is a stranger, this could well be your future Twin Flame; but the dream could also point to unexplored potential within you.

Déjà rêvé. On your Twin Flame Path, you may start to dream of things that manifest in your waking life – a phenomenon called *déjà rêvé*, or 'dream remembered'. Perhaps you dream of a conversation or a place that later manifests in real life; or you might dream of someone you have not heard from in years and then they text you out of the blue the following day. These precognitive dreams highlight the divinely orchestrated nature of your Divine Union and reassure you that everything is unfolding as it should.

Case Study: Maya's Twin Flame Dream Journey

Let's take a deeper look at the dreamwork of Maya, a woman who experienced precognitive dreams and internal guidance long before meeting her Twin Flame in real life. Maya had been exploring her spiritual path for many years when she first began experiencing dreams that seemed to defy logic and explanation. For years, Maya had felt a profound yearning – a sense that something important was missing from her life, even though she had a successful career and fulfilling friendships.

Maya's dreams began as fragmented and unclear but grew more vivid over time. In one, she found herself walking down a cobblestone street at dusk, feeling an overwhelming sense of peace. As she rounded the corner, a woman stood waiting for her. Maya felt an instant recognition – a deep, soul-level knowing that this person was meant to be in her life. The woman's face was shrouded in light and Maya did not recognize her, but the connection between them was undeniable.

For years, Maya didn't understand these dreams, dismissing them as symbolic rather than prophetic. It wasn't until she met Jane – who had a similar aura of recognition and a sense of homecoming – that she realized that her dreams had been preparing her for their union.

At the beginning of their relationship, Maya experienced a range of dreams reflecting both the beauty and the challenges of their connection. Some dreams depicted perfect harmony – an image of the two of them sitting in a garden, hand in hand, surrounded by golden light. Others depicted emotional struggle, with the two of them drifting apart or facing internal battles. These dreams mirrored their relationship struggles and helped Maya navigate the emotional rollercoaster of their connection.

Eventually, Maya's dreams began to shift. As she worked through her own emotional healing and growth, her dreams evolved into more peaceful and spiritual union-like experiences. She used these dreams to gain clarity and insight into her own personal transformation, as well as the necessary spiritual work required for her to fully align with the energy of Divine Union.

What Are Dreams?

In my humble opinion, dreams are messages from your heart and the language spoken by your intuition and creativity. They are not random firings of the brain. Studies show they are a sign of holistic wellbeing and can help you with problem-solving, boost memory and creativity and offer stress relief. Best of all, consistently keeping a dream journal can help you understand yourself better, because your dreams really do shine the nightlight on your current mindset and whether it's helping or hindering you in your waking life. Understanding yourself is the beginning of all wisdom.

You may think that you don't dream, but you do. Brain scans show that we all dream at least five or six times a night – so you're just not recalling your dreams. Below, you will find some simple things you can do to improve your dream recall. And if the roadblock is that you are not understanding the meaning of your dreams, there are simple techniques to help you interpret their personal meaning too.

How to Recall and Understand the Meaning of Your Dreams

Before you go to sleep, put your phone away somewhere that is not your bedside, so it's not within arm's reach on waking.

Place a pen and piece of paper or a notebook with blank pages right by your bed. If it's going to be dark when you wake up, a torch or nightlight is advised. Make sure these things are in within arm's reach on waking. If you prefer, you can also use a voice recorder.

Rest your head on your pillow and, as you drift off to sleep, tell yourself you're going to recall your dreams on waking. Your mind is very impressionable just before you fall asleep and immediately after you wake up. Tell yourself you want your dreams to guide you on your Twin Flame Journey.

When you wake in the morning (or in the night), keep still with your eyes closed for at least a minute or so and recall your dreams, or the feelings and images associated with them. Send unconditional love to your heart and to every other part of your body.

When symbols, images, stories, feelings surface in your mind, sit up, reach for your pen and paper and write them down. Don't try to make them make sense. Simply thank your unconscious for its wisdom and for reminding you that you have an inner world. Let that wisdom settle and trust that it will bring clarity when the time is right for you. Dream decoding is always better done with the benefit of hindsight, so avoid trying to force meanings first thing and instead return to your dream journal later in the day, or when you have the time to reflect.

Let your dreaming mind know you've heard it and are going to take it seriously. One way to do this is to use the power of action. Choose a harmless and gentle aspect of a dream, such as a colour or an object, and then live out that aspect during the day. For example, if there were flowers in your dream, you could buy yourself a bunch of flowers. If any more recollections arise later in the day, write them down too. See what associations and connections they trigger and if there's anything from your dream you can safely re-create in your waking life. Live your dream.

If you wake and can't recall a dream, it's still important to reach for your dream journal because how you feel on waking will be inspired by the dreams you had and this may trigger memories. Write down the words 'I feel', and if nothing else comes to mind then continue to document your waking thoughts and feelings.

During the day, watch your stress levels and make sure you get plenty of the dream-recall vitamin B6 in your diet. B6 is found in sunflower seeds, tuna, turkey and dried fruit. Reading fiction, a spot of video gaming, plenty of meditation and giving yourself permission to daydream can all ignite clearer dream recall too. Above all, don't panic: everyone goes through periods when they don't recall their dreams. Simply trust that when the time is right, you'll start to remember them again.

Dreams speak the language of the unconscious, which is the symbolic language of the poet and the artist. To better understand them – and therefore yourself – you need to connect to your inner visionary and explore the deeper meaning beneath the surface of things. Dreams aren't linear, direct, literal or logical. For example, if you dream your teeth are falling out, you might consider in which area of your life you've been feeling 'toothless' recently, or whether you're concerned about appearance or ageing.

Remember too that your dreams dramatize your current mindset and what's helping or hindering your personal growth. Every aspect of the dream symbolizes an aspect of yourself and your perspective, as your dreams are created by you, for you, and are all about you. If you don't like how your dreams make you feel on waking, they can serve as an awesome reminder of the power of personal choice. You get to choose how you think, feel and react; if you don't like how your choices make you feel, you always have the power within you to makes changes now.

Dreams are a fantastic tool for greater self-awareness and there are plenty of books out there (I should know, as I've written several) to help you learn how to use them as self-help tools and creativity hacks. Why not invest some time in learning more about dreams and by implication yourself? You won't regret it.

Instead of reaching for your mobile on waking, and letting its outside-in demands drain your energy, spending a few minutes writing down your dreams and reflecting on their meaning is one of the greatest self-help gifts you can give yourself. Notice how liberated this activity makes you feel and how it ignites an awareness of your own worth and uniqueness, a sense of yourself as being mysterious and interesting. A sense of yourself independent of external validation. There truly is a treasure trove of inner creativity in the wonderland of your own dreams. Plunder and brainstorm them for a sense of deep meaning and direction and to help you attract your Twin Flame. And to help you decode the heart of your dreams a few important decoding reminders:

> **You, unfiltered.** Dreams act as a symbolic reflection of your unconscious landscape, revealing patterns, fears, desires and unresolved wounds. When you get into the habit of recalling your dreams, and learn how to interpret and understand what they are showing you, you can use their insight and their honesty to help you move through your Twin Flame Journey with greater clarity and self-awareness. Your unconscious or dreaming mind does not filter, lie or censor; it brings to the surface emotions, thoughts and experiences that you may not even be aware of in your waking life but which you need to confront for your personal growth. Interpreting these dreams is an invaluable tool for self-awareness, as they give you access to the hidden parts of yourself – the parts that may need healing, attention, or simply compassion and a shift in perspective for you to move forward.
>
> **Identifying emotional patterns.** Dreams often symbolically highlight recurring emotional patterns – both positive and negative – that you may not recognize in your waking

life because your ego is blocking them from your conscious awareness. If you often dream of feeling abandoned or rejected, for example, this could indicate unresolved emotional wounds related to feelings of unworthiness or past relationships. These dreams are an invitation to explore these feelings, understand their origin and heal them so that they do not interfere with your Divine Union. Notice the emotional tone of your dreams – whether they are peaceful, anxiety-filled, or steeped in longing – as their meaning is most likely to be found in those emotions. The more you can identify the emotional patterns within your dreams, the better you can begin to address them consciously, shifting those patterns in your waking life.

Understanding relationship dynamics. Your relationships, both past and present, often show up symbolically in your dreams, offering valuable insights into the dynamics that are affecting your Twin Flame Evolution. Remember that people who appear in your dreams more often than not symbolize an aspect of yourself that you need to understand better. For example, if you dream of an ex-partner who causes emotional pain, this could be a sign that there is still emotional work to be done regarding past wounds or lessons learned from that relationship. It is not a sign you want them back. They are an ex for a reason. If you dream of having an affair, this could suggest you need to inject more passion and adventure into your life and your relationship, if you are in one. Alternatively, positive dreams about friends or family members might indicate the types of supportive relationships or personality traits you need to cultivate to help your Cosmic Love flourish.

Healing your inner child. Dreams that feature childhood memories, figures from your past, or vulnerable and neglected people or animals can be reflections of your inner child's desires and fears. By paying attention to these dreams, you can clearly identify limiting patterns of fear, abandonment, or self-doubt that may have been carried into your adult life and relationships. Through dreamwork, you can actively engage in healing your inner child, offering comfort, compassion and emotional safety to those parts of yourself that need it. These practices can help you parent yourself and lead to shifts in how you approach your Twin Flame Journey, allowing you to approach your Divine Union with greater self-awareness and self-love.

Jungian Dream Analysis

One powerful way to interpret your dreams is through the lens of Carl Jung's analytical psychology. As previously mentioned (see page 101), this framework emphasizes the importance of the unconscious in the process of individuation – the journey towards becoming a whole, integrated self which is the foundation stone of your Twin Flame Odyssey.

Individuation, you may recall, involves becoming the true or authentic Self, integrating the conscious and unconscious aspects of the psyche. The Twin Flame Awakening is intrinsically linked to the process of individuation, as both partners must become whole within themselves before they can fully reunite.

Through dream analysis, you can identify where you are in your individuation process and gain clarity about what work still needs to be done to reach full union.

Jung believed that dreams were messages from the unconscious, revealing both personal and collective aspects of the Self. In the context of Cosmic Love, Jungian analysis can therefore help you identify unconscious patterns, archetypes and symbolic representations of the Self and the other, all of which will contribute to your understanding of your Twin Flame.

Archetypes, according to Jung, are universal symbols and patterns that reside within the collective unconscious or within everyone. Dreams about your Twin Flame often bring up archetypal figures, such as the child, the lover, the anima/animus (see page 91), and understanding how and why these archetypes appear can help you navigate your Divine Union with greater awareness and clarity.

Be aware that the Twin Flame Journey often activates the shadow archetype, triggering unconscious fears, insecurities and emotional wounds that can manifest in nightmares of conflict, rejection, panic, or fear. Nightmares are not to be feared but should be better understood. They are transformative gifts that help you acknowledge your shadow and cathartically release limiting beliefs and emotional blocks that stand in the way of your union.

Practical Dream Exercises for the Twin Flame Journey

Dream Journalling

Keep a dream journal by your bedside and write down your dreams as soon as you wake up. Even if you don't remember all the details, write down whatever you can (refer back to the discussion on page 206 if you need to). Over time, patterns, symbols and themes will emerge. Review your journal regularly to track your emotional and spiritual growth throughout your Twin Flame Adventure.

Nighttime Intention Setting (Dream Incubation)

Before bed, set a specific intention for your dreams that is related to your Divine Union. For example:

> 'I am open to receiving insight into the next step of my Twin Flame Journey.'
>
> 'I invite guidance in understanding the emotional work I need to do for healing my relationship with myself and with others.'

Write this intention in a journal or say it aloud before sleep. This practice helps your subconscious mind focus on your desired outcome. (See also the 'Dreaming Your Twin Flame into Being' exercise on the following page.)

Active Imagination

Inspired by Jungian techniques, active imagination is a way of engaging with dream images and symbols while you are awake. After a dream, sit quietly and visualize yourself in the dream scene. Engage with the dream characters, asking questions or exploring the emotions you felt. This can bring richer insights into your unconscious motivations and guide you towards healing.

Dream Reframing

If you have a particularly challenging or distressing dream about your Twin Flame, try consciously reframing it. Imagine or write down an alternative ending or outcome where the conflict is resolved, or the emotional tension is healed. This practice helps shift the energy of the dream and can provide healing and emotional resolution.

Exercise: Dreaming Your Twin Flame into Being

Purpose: This dream-incubation technique will help you connect with your Spiritual Mirror in the dream realm, especially if you haven't yet met them in the physical world.

Thirty minutes or so before you go to sleep at night, find a quiet space and close your eyes. Take a few deep breaths to relax. Then, repeat the following affirmation out loud or silently:

> 'I invite my Twin Flame to meet me in my dreams tonight. I trust that my soul will recognize them and that I will awaken with clarity and understanding.'

Visualize a connection between your soul and your Twin Flame, even if you've never met them before. Picture yourself standing at the beginning of a glowing bridge of light. Walk along it until you reach the end, where a figure stands. This is your Twin Flame. Feel the warmth and love between you. Let any messages or emotions flow naturally and trust that your soul recognizes them.

If you struggle to visualize, grab a pen and paper and write down a paragraph or two describing the meeting.

Then, when you are in bed and your head is on your pillow, just before you fall asleep, say to yourself out loud if you can:

> 'Tonight, I will meet my Twin Flame in my dreams. I trust this connection and will remember it clearly upon waking.'

Upon waking, immediately write down anything you remember from your dream, especially any images, feelings, or encounters. Jot down any symbols or emotional insights, even if you didn't meet your Spiritual Mirror directly, as these may contain important associations. As previously indicated, if you struggle with recall, write down how you are feeling.

Later the same day, ask for guidance and clarity and re-read your dream notes. See what insights come – but do be patient with yourself if none surface, because you can always dream another dream. Go through all possible meanings in your mind until your intuition draws you to one and you get a 'eureka moment'. The mark of a dream correctly decoded is that it will raise you up or inspire you with a surprising new perspective. Dreams love to tell you something new about yourself. If the interpretation drags you down, it is not the correct interpretation.

Ask for further guidance or clarity and stay open to signs or synchronicities in your daily life that have been foreshadowed in your dreams. Contrary to what you may think, you are still you when you dream – you have just entered a different state of consciousness. Your dreaming life and waking life constantly comment on and influence each other.

The more you focus on your dream meanings and look for signs in your waking life, the more revelations your dreams will reveal. The dream world can be a powerful space to connect with your Twin Flame before meeting them in the physical world. Stay consistent with this practice and allow your soul to guide the way.

Your Nocturnal Guide

The Twin Flame Journey is a profoundly transformative process that stretches you beyond your limits and calls you to grow in ways you never imagined. Dreams can serve as sacred guides on this path, offering you much needed illumination, hope and healing along the way. Through repeatedly interpreting your dreams, brainstorming the meaning of their symbolic language, you can unlock powerful emotional and spiritual truths, guiding you towards ever-greater self-awareness, deeper relationships and Divine Union.

With dreamwork, the emphasis is on repetition. You need to establish a pattern of regular dream recall every morning on waking before their meanings will become clear. This is because your dreams are like a long-running series that you need to tune into every night to continue the amazing inside-out story of you. Too many people focus all their attention on one particularly vivid dream, forgetting that the dialogue we have with our dreams is ongoing. Over time, if you keep writing down your dreams and, most importantly, revisiting your dream journal with the benefit of hindsight, you will start to see that they are like an ever-present symbolic voiceover or commentary on your waking life. They are constantly offering you brainstorming connections and insights about things in your waking life that your intuition knows are important for your personal and spiritual growth – and therefore your Twin Flame Odyssey – but that your waking mind is ignoring.

I do hope this chapter has inspired you to never let another dream memory slip away and to consider committing to a long-term relationship with your dreaming mind, rather than a one-night stand. Write down your dreams on waking and reflect on their meaning. Use them as tools for your emotional healing, self-growth and spiritual alignment and trust in the wisdom they offer.

May your dreams guide you to Cosmic Love, and may they bring you closer to the divine love and wholeness that await you on your Twin Flame Journey.

Note: Dreamwork is my passion, so do feel free to contact me if you are new to it and want a little extra advice about the meaning of a specific dream to help you get started. Details of how to get in touch (whether for dream-decoding advice or with questions about anything you encounter on your Twin Flame Journey) can be found on page 295.

6

UNREQUITED LOVE

Maybe you're in love with someone who can't return that love – or, at least, not in the way you need. The pain of unrequited love is one of the most intense and brutal experiences of the human condition. It can feel like your heart is torn between longing and despair, and it often seems impossible to find any peace in it.

But here's the truth: though painful, unrequited romantic love is a profound gateway to understanding yourself and what true love is. It is not the end of your Twin Flame Journey. It can be the beginning, middle and end. As you read this chapter, do bear in mind that unrequited love is distinct from other intimate relationships you may encounter on your pilgrimage to higher love, whether they are Karmic, False Flames or Soul Mates. Those relationships may well involve their fair share of heartbreak, and the sorrow of love given but not returned, but unrequited love is generally different because it refers to a love that is entirely one-sided and not reciprocated. More often than not, the other party will not acknowledge your feelings or even give you the opportunity to discuss them together. In other words, the harsh reality of unrequited love is that the person you think you are in love with does not feel the same way about you – or, if the relationship was previously set in motion, they have since decided to stop returning your feelings or being a part of your life.

As this book has made clear so far, the Twin Flame Path is not entirely about finding someone who will complete you. It's about recognizing that you are already complete and that your Twin Flame Journey is simply a reflection of that completeness. Before you can attract your Spiritual Mirror – or even recognize them when they arrive – you must first cultivate a deep, authentic love for yourself. This is easier said than done when your heart is aching.

The Gift of Heartbreak

Unrequited love – love that is not returned, no matter how much you give – is utterly heart- and soul-wrenching. It can leave you feeling empty, rejected and unsure of where to turn next. The weight of unrequited love presses down on you, making it hard to focus on anything else. You may find yourself replaying every conversation, wondering what went wrong, or questioning what you did or didn't do, or why the person of your dreams isn't into you.

But what if this heartache is not a curse but a blessing in disguise? What if it's not the end of the story but a course correction, pointing you in the direction of something much more profound – something that will transform you from the inside out? Remember, the Twin Flame Awakening is not about finding the 'perfect person' – someone who will complete you, make you feel whole and fill the void inside. It is you becoming the version of yourself who is ready to attract and receive the higher love and Divine Union you deserve.

The pain of unrequited love can reveal where you're still seeking love outside of yourself, rather than cultivating it from within. The journey through unrequited love can ultimately bring you closer to your true self, helping you to build a foundation of unshakable self-love. This, in turn, will prepare you for Cosmic Love, whether that manifests with another person or within yourself.

By the end of this chapter, you will learn how to turn the experience of unreturned love into an opportunity for self-healing and bliss. I'll guide you through the process of transforming your broken heart into art and your pain into personal power and purpose. You'll learn how embracing the depths of despair really can be a transformative gift and open the door to your higher love.

Love Happens?

Love is your birthright. It is your essence. Everybody can love and deserves to be loved. It is something we all need and want. But the biggest mistake we make about love is thinking that it simply happens, or that we need to wait for it to strike. This belief means that when we encounter someone our hormones go wild for, we can mistake that physical or biological lust for love. For two people who are compatible, such an encounter may flower into a beautiful coupling; but often it doesn't and our hearts get broken, again and again, until we learn that love is a personal choice we make in any given moment. It is a personal choice because being loved by someone else does not make you lovable. The only way to truly feel lovable is to choose to feel loving from within.

You must become the love you seek. True love is always an internal decision.

Relationships can teach you about love and offer temporary relief, but at the end of the day the love you feel will always reflect how much love you have for yourself. If you can nurture your own emotional needs, you don't crave for others to fulfil them for you. This emotional self-sufficiency enables you to rise above the 'love is blind' stage to see others clearly, find someone who is right for or compatible with you and then enjoy celebrating them for who they are, not for who you want them to be. That is the template for a healthy and fulfilling Divine Union. No expectations.

When you love yourself in a healthy way, your intimate relationship is not built on dependency, duty or expectation; it's built on unconditional love. You are walking your Twin Flame Journey towards the person that aligns with you because you have returned to the self-love that is your birthright and something you can consciously choose. Yet many of us have simply not been taught that self-love is our birthright. For whatever reason, our parents, carers, teachers and society have not told us that we can make that decision, or how to make it.

Self-Love, Again!

True love is something many of us feel cynical about because of our experiences in the School of Hard Knocks. But it doesn't have to be that way. Anyone can learn this essential true-love hack at any time. You don't need to get your heart broken or be overwhelmed by feelings of grief and emptiness before you learn it.

Self-love is not a cliché. It's not just a feel-good idea or about indulging in temporary pleasures or convincing yourself that you're worthy through affirmations and make-overs. True self-love is rooted in self-acceptance and self-awareness. It's the understanding that you are enough as you are and that your value doesn't depend on how anyone else feels about you. Being authentic and celebrating your true self, 'warts and all', is the bedrock on which your Twin Flame Voyage is built.

Self-love is an essential practice for attracting loving energy into your life. The more you love yourself, the more you can attract a partner who reflects that same love back to you. Lack of self-love is what keeps people stuck in toxic, unfulfilling relationships – including those characterized by unrequited love, where you are longing for someone but they don't long for you, or you are chasing someone and they are running from you.

But self-love is not a one-time achievement – it's a lifelong practice that requires you to continuously check in with yourself every day and honour your needs, desires and boundaries. It's a commitment to treating yourself with the same care, compassion and respect that you would offer to your Twin Flame should they appear in your life.

You probably know deep down that self-love is important. But were you ever taught how to love yourself in a healthy way? No time like the present. Here's how to get started. If you are amid any kind of heartbreak right now – whether it's because of rejection, dumping, ghosting, divorce, a False Flame encounter, or a love scam – flag this section of the book and return to it repeatedly. Keep coming back here until you make a conscious decision to implement the recommendations outlined, because they offer you an astonishing opportunity to transform your heartbreak into inner strength and wisdom. Without these lessons firmly in place – or at the very least an awareness of their importance and the need to relentlessly practise them – there really is little point reading the rest of this book.

Love and Grief

The following recommendations in this chapter can also apply if you are enduring the anguish of bereavement. Although nothing can immediately diminish the pain of grief, with the passing of time the death of a loved one can offer you a chance to awaken spiritually.

The passing of a loved one is a big spiritual wake-up call, a reminder that death ends a life on Earth but not a relationship. If you have ever lost a loved one, you will know that the invisible bond of love created between you can never be broken; while you can't explain how or why, you know that part of them remains alive. You can continue to sense or feel them through dreams, memories and afterlife signs or synchronicities that let you know they are still watching over and loving you.

Knowing how to nurture this ongoing relationship with someone you have loved and lost, whether or not they are your Spiritual Mirror, matters greatly on your Twin Flame Pilgrimage, because the 'crisis' of bereavement touches us all at some point in our lives. We will therefore revisit this subject later (see page 269). For now, though, let your mind and heart

> ponder the metaphor below. If what you read or hear gives you goosebumps, you will know its enduring truth and that it is something you are meant to remember.
>
> When someone you love dies, they don't just help you understand that there is more to this life than the physical body; they also give you the greatest and most unconditionally loving gift of all, which is the opportunity to reclaim the love you gave them and return it to the place where it has always belonged – your heart.
>
> That is why, when you have grieved their physical passing and found yourself in a place where you can think of them with a smile before a tear, you will often feel not empty but warm and glowing from the inside out whenever you remember them. This is a surefire sign that your love for them and their love for you have merged in spirit and found a lasting home in your heart. And that love lives on forever within you, having become a force of infinite strength and wisdom you can tap into at any time on your Twin Flame Journey.

Acknowledge Your Worth

First and foremost, acknowledge your worth, even if you don't feel like it.

We often seek love and approval from others because we feel a deep need to be validated. But your worth is not determined by someone else's approval or affection. Your worth is inherent; it's a part of who you are at the core of your being. Start by regularly affirming your own value. This can be as simple as looking in the mirror each morning and saying, with your thoughts or out loud:

'I am worthy of love and I am deserving of happiness.'

Even if you don't fully believe it at first, repeat this daily. Over time, your subconscious will begin to accept it as truth. And, yes, mirror work is a self-help cliché – but, like many clichés, it is true and it can be beneficial.

And don't stop at thoughts and words; make sure your daily actions match those words. There is no point telling yourself that you matter and then minimizing yourself during the day. There is no point telling yourself you are going to prioritize yourself and then neglecting to practise self-care. There is no point telling yourself you are enough and then only feeling good when someone else notices and praises you. If your self-esteem relies totally on the opinions of others – and there is no easy way to say this – your self-esteem is non-existent.

Forgive Yourself

So often, we carry the weight of past mistakes and regrets, which can prevent us from truly loving ourselves. It is easy to blame yourself if the love you are giving to someone else isn't being returned or valued. The Twin Flame Journey is rooted in forgiveness – not only of others but of ourselves too. When you forgive yourself, you release the energetic blockages that prevent new love from flowing into your life. You are allowed to make mistakes; you are allowed to heal. Self-forgiveness is the gift you must consciously give yourself if you want to move forward. Ask yourself: 'What part of me still needs healing?' 'What part of me needs compassion?'

Nurture Yourself

Give yourself the care and attention you deserve. This is more than just treating yourself to a spa day; it's about nourishing your body, mind and heart, not just now and again but consistently, every day. What does your soul crave? Maybe it's more rest, better nutrition, or time to engage in hobbies that bring you joy. Self-care is about responding to the needs of your inner self and treating yourself as you would treat someone you love dearly.

Set Boundaries

Setting healthy boundaries doesn't mean shutting others out; it means honouring your own emotional needs first. This will show the universe that you value yourself and that you feel worthy of love.

One of the most important lessons in unrequited love is learning to set boundaries. If you're emotionally attached to someone who is not reciprocating your feelings, you've got to draw a line in the sand between them and you and create space for yourself to heal. This may involve taking a step back from communication with that person and the energy you give them with your thoughts. You need to stop chasing the potential, see the reality and take your power back.

Establish clear boundaries around how much energy you give to someone who isn't fully present in the relationship. This isn't about being cold or unkind; it's about prioritizing your emotional wellbeing. Boundaries are acts of self-love – they protect your heart and allow you to focus on healing.

Above all, just let go of the expectation that you can control what other adults in your life say, think, or feel about you. You can't. You can't control the reactions of others. You can't make someone love you. Let them live their lives the way they want to live them; let them think or feel about you what they will; and let them give their love to whoever they decide to give it to. Focus only on what you can control, which is your love, your perspective and your response.

Step away from relationships with people who don't commit or value you as you deserve.

Letting go is tough when your relationship is clearly one-sided and you are doing all the work, because you have invested so much of yourself into a potential that doesn't exist and you don't want all that personal energy to be wasted. But it must be done – and nothing has been wasted as long as you learn from it. If the two of you can't work things out, or if your partner is unwilling to give to the relationship as much as you do, leave.

But what if your relationship is one where you both care about each other but you know, deep down, that you are putting on a mask; that you aren't right for them and they aren't right for you? If this is the case, you need more time and reflection, please. You need to talk to your partner and explain to them what you feel is missing from your relationship, or what it is that you want them to change. Give them a chance to show you they have heard you – but if they don't change, it is time to say goodbye. It is easier said than done, but in some cases having the 'talk' is the best thing that could happen to your relationship:

your partner may realize it is a deal-breaker and may try harder to respect your feelings because they don't want to lose you. And if your partner is simply unable to adjust their behaviour on your behalf, you need to decide whether you can love them exactly as they are – not for who you wish they could be. If you can't do that, the relationship has run its course.

The key question to ask yourself is: do you want to spend the rest of your life with this person if they don't change? If the answer is that you don't know, or that you know you can't love and accept the person as they are – without feeling resentment for them or compromising too much on what matters to you – then it is time to part ways and for you to concentrate on reclaiming the part of your heart that you gave away.

Relationships end for all sorts of reasons and this is never going to be an easy decision to make; but the harsh truth is that if you are with someone you love but who does not love you for who you are, or with someone who does not want to work on the relationship to make it stronger, you need to end the relationship before it ends you.

Note: If, like me, you are in a relationship where you are caring for someone who is vulnerable, or has poor physical and/or mental health, and who, through no fault of their own, simply can't give you what you need, you may be unable or unwilling to leave them because they are dependent on your care. Should this be the case for you, please know that you are not stuck or alone. Even though you may feel obligated to stay and care for them, this situation can be reframed as part of your

Twin Flame Adventure. This could become an opportunity for you to transform your challenging circumstances into something deeply meaningful, potentially helping you evolve and discover an inner strength and love you didn't know you had.

Case Study: Grant and David

Grant had always felt a deep sense of knowing that he had met his Spiritual Mirror in David. The connection was undeniable – electric, passionate and at times overwhelming. The chemistry between them was intense, and they shared moments that felt like they were cut from a different reality. Yet, as much as Grant poured his heart into the relationship, David couldn't meet him at the same emotional depth. He enjoyed the connection but wasn't ready to fully commit.

For months, Grant felt heartbroken, confused and desperate for answers. He couldn't understand why David seemed distant and unsure about their future together. He tried everything – changing his approach, becoming more patient, more understanding – but nothing seemed to shift. Eventually, he came to a painful realization: no matter how much love he offered, David couldn't reciprocate it in the way he needed.

Frustrated, Grant decided to focus on himself. He took a break from David and poured his energy into self-care. He started journalling, practising meditation and reaffirming his worth. Slowly but surely, he began to heal. Through this process, he realized that his love for himself was more important than his desire to be loved by someone who wasn't ready to give him the love he deserved.

As Grant worked on his self-love and healing, he became more confident, peaceful and whole. Over time, he realized that whether David reciprocated his feelings or not, he was still worthy of love and deserving of a fulfilling life. Interestingly, as Grant's focus shifted away from David and onto his own growth, David began to show signs of emotional openness. But by then, Grant had discovered a new level of self-worth – although the change delighted him, he was no longer reliant on David's affection to feel whole.

Moving Through the Pain of Unrequited Love

Unrequited love strips you raw. The more you give and the less you receive, the more depleted you feel and, bizarrely, the more addicted you get to chasing the love and the pain of it. But the pain you feel is not a punishment – it's an invitation to plunge deeper than ever before into self-awareness. It teaches you about the places where you may still be seeking validation from others and provides the space and opportunity for you to reclaim your sense of self-worth.

When all is said and done, working through the pain of unreturned love is one seriously tough challenge. The idea of valuing yourself and loving yourself more makes sense, but these things are rather hard to do when you feel out of love and your heart is running on empty. Here are some pointers to help you emerge stronger and wiser from your grief.

Feel the Pain

When you realize that your love is not reciprocated, you may experience a range of intense emotions: sadness, anger, confusion and even betrayal. Being told at this time to love yourself more will fall on deaf ears and a closed heart, because you probably don't feel great about yourself as your heart shatters into pieces. You may well question the merit of everything, even things that you know deep down are true.

You are grieving the loss of someone who felt like they were a part of you – or like they *should* be a part of you, if you have adored someone from afar. There will be memories everywhere. And the best thing to do, especially in the early days, is to avoid contact with them or reminders of them as much as possible. Remove physical reminders and triggers and then take things one day and one small step at a time.

First and foremost, allow yourself to grieve. It's natural to feel heartbroken when you love someone who does not feel the same way, or who has left your life for whatever reason. Don't suppress or bottle up these emotions. They are valid and have much they want to tell you or teach you; processing them is an essential part of healing.

Give yourself permission to feel everything fully – without shame or self-judgment. Take time to sit with your emotions, even if they are uncomfortable. Allow yourself the space to cry, express your frustration, scream, punch a cushion or even vent to a trusted friend or therapist. The goal is not to stay in the pain but to cathartically release it and then move through it. The more you allow yourself to fully process your feelings, the quicker you will heal and shift into a higher state of self-awareness.

It's tempting to bury the pain of unrequited love, but this only prolongs the healing process. The first step in healing a broken heart is always to allow yourself to feel the full weight of your emotions. Don't suppress your grief, anger, or confusion. Grief is a natural response to unrequited love. Feel the sadness, anger, frustration and confusion without judgment. These intense and often painful emotions are part of the process. But remember: feeling your emotions is not the same as being consumed by them. Acknowledge them, but then gently remind yourself that even though you feel sad you are still whole and worthy of love. The fact that you *feel* angry or sad does not mean you *are* angry or sad. It just means that feelings of anger and sadness are passing through you. Sit with the discomfort and understand that your emotions are signals, not obstacles; lessons, not punishment. They are there to teach you much of value about yourself and the meaning of true love.

Shift Your Perspective

After you've allowed yourself to have a big cry, the next step is to begin seeing the pain of unrequited love as an opportunity for growth. Again, this is easier said than done, so give yourself time. Instead of viewing the experience as a failure, or a sign that you are unworthy, reframe it. This person is not the one who completes you – your relationship with yourself is calling your name now to remind you that this is always what matters most.

You may not feel like it right now, but never forget that you are always the love you are seeking. Being in a relationship does not make you worthy of experiencing love. Your life does – and the true love of your life will always be you. Think about it. There is only one person in your life who is going to be with you in every moment and wake up every morning with you – and that person is you. You are born alone and you die alone; and the most important relationship is always the one you have with yourself.

Use this time to reflect on what you have learned from the situation. Relationships can be a source of great joy, and you deserve the very best relationship, but the genesis of everything is the way you treat and feel about yourself. What recurring patterns have you noticed in your past relationships? What do you still need to heal and find within yourself? What are you seeking externally that you need to seek within?

This isn't about becoming selfish or self-centred. Quite the opposite. It is about recognizing that the love you give yourself is the model that all your relationships draw their inspiration and energy from. This book has made it abundantly clear that you don't need other people to give you love, validation, support or to help you make your dreams come true. Only you can give you all of that. How you choose to love yourself creates the life and the relationships that you attract with that self-love. From now on, when it comes to your relationships, don't ever accept less than you feel you deserve. Love people for who they are and do the same for yourself. Never ever forget that you choose how love reveals itself in your life.

Let your heartbreak be the breakthrough you need to finally understand that you have zero control over someone else's heart. If they are sending you signals that you are not their priority, stop chasing. And if they do love you but can't be with you physically for whatever reason, let them go too. The greatest love is the love that can let go. If you try to trap a butterfly in your hand, you will crush it. If you cage a wild bird, you clip its wings. If you truly love someone, you want them to be happy and free – even if that means it is without you. Focus entirely now on connecting to the love within you and reminding yourself of your own power to choose what you want to think, feel, say and do next. You get to choose to make yourself happy, not someone else.

Mindfulness Practice

Mindfulness is the practice of being present with your thoughts, emotions and sensations without judgment. By practising mindfulness, you create a space between your feelings and your reactions. When you're consumed by the pain of unrequited love, mindfulness can dramatically help you detach from the intensity of your emotions, allowing you to observe them without getting lost in them.

Consider incorporating meditation, yoga, or deep-breathing exercises into your routine to help calm your mind. You might find it helpful to practise a little more gratitude as well. Take a moment each day to reflect on the things you are grateful for – your health, your friends, your talents and your ability to grow. Gratitude shifts your focus from what is lacking to what is abundant in your life.

Transform Pain into Purpose

Pain that is processed has the potential to transform into personal power. As you heal from unrequited love, begin to invest more of your energy and time into things that uplift and empower you. Start practising daily rituals that nourish your soul – whether that's reading, listening to music or spending time in nature. The more you focus on filling your own cup, the more your energy will shift from one of lack to one of abundance. As you heal, you'll find that you naturally begin to attract healthier, more aligned connections into your life.

When you're caught in the cycle of yearning for someone who doesn't reciprocate, your self-care tends to fall away. Now, more than ever, it's so very important to nurture yourself. This doesn't just mean taking bubble baths or treating yourself to your favourite meal; it means engaging in forms of self-care that are personal- and spiritual-growth tools, such as journalling, meditating, or dreamwork, which this book has already championed. The more you care for yourself, the more the pain will begin to shift from grief to growth.

Affirm Your Self-Worth

Another damaging aspect of unrequited love is the belief that you are somehow unworthy or undeserving of love. You may wonder: 'What's wrong with me? Why isn't this person able to see my value?' Once again, it's critical to recognize that your worth should never be determined by another person's feelings towards you. You are worthy of love, simply because you exist. End of.

Another reminder here to set a daily practice of reaffirming your worth. Look into that mirror again and again and say, out loud or with your thoughts:

> 'I am enough. I am worthy of love, respect and kindness.'

Write down a list of qualities that make you unique, beautiful and lovable – whether it's your kindness, your creativity, your resilience, or your sense of humour. This practice can help rebuild your self-esteem, reminding you that you are whole and lovable, independent of another person's approval.

Master the Art of Detachment

Detachment is one of the hardest lessons to learn on the Twin Flame Path. When you are deeply invested in someone's love and approval, it's easy to get lost in the belief that your happiness depends on their decisions. Detachment doesn't mean shutting off your feelings for them; rather, it means recognizing that your peace and joy should never ever depend on someone else's decision to love you. True detachment is about becoming whole within yourself and finding contentment in solitude. It is about releasing your expectations of others and what is outside your control and focusing on what is within your control: your thoughts, your feelings, your actions.

The only way to fully understand just how healing and empowering detachment can be is to apply it in your daily life, especially during times of emotional crisis. The detachment and observer ritual exercises below can help you break free from emotional attachment and gain clarity during heartbreak or unrequited love.

Twin Flame Ritual: Detachment

Before beginning this ritual, find a quiet, comfortable space where you can reflect and not be disturbed. This could be a favourite corner of your home, a peaceful outdoor setting, or any place where you feel safe and grounded.

First, set an intention for your journey of detachment. This could be something like:

'I am learning to let go with grace.'
Or:
'I choose to release what no longer serves me.'

Write this intention down on a piece of paper or say it out loud, connecting deeply with the sentiment behind the words.

Take a few moments to write a letter to the person you're feeling attached to, whether they are someone you are heartbroken over or someone you feel unrequited love for. This letter is not for them; it's for you. When you write, be honest about the depth of your emotions. Let them spill out on the page. Even if it hurts, find something you are grateful for in the experience (growth, lessons, even the love that once existed). Then verbally release the connection, acknowledging that it no longer serves you in a healthy way. After that, symbolically express this release by tearing up your letter, visualizing the fragments as pieces of the attachment you're letting go of. You can also burn the letter, if it's safe to do so, or bury it in the ground; or you can let it drift away in a body of water, symbolizing the letting go of old energy.

With compassion, say to yourself:

'I release you, but I don't release myself. I am still whole. I choose to heal, I choose to move on and I choose to love myself fully.'

This act of self-compassion reinforces your sense of self-worth and acknowledges that your healing is not dependent on someone else.

End the exercise by visualizing or describing with your thoughts the person you want to become: the empowered, healed version of yourself, free from the past attachment. Imagine yourself fully content, independent and open to new opportunities in love and life.

This ritual will take you through the emotional and symbolic act of letting go. Detachment is not about hardening your heart or losing your capacity to love; it's about decluttering your mind and heart and creating space for healing and growth. It's a tool to help you move forward and free yourself from the grip of heartbreak, opening yourself to the future with clarity and hope.

Twin Flame Ritual: The Observer Effect

Practising detachment by stepping into the role of observer during a crisis can be incredibly challenging, but it's also one of the most powerful ways to manage your emotional response and regain a sense of control. This doesn't mean ignoring or not caring; it means recognizing that you don't have to be fully consumed by the situation. You can rise above it and see the bigger picture.

This exercise helps create space between you and the chaos around you. It's about acknowledging that you can respond rather than react – there's a difference between being swept away by a storm and being the calm centre in its eye.

> Take a few minutes to be alone in a quiet space where you won't be disturbed. You don't need a special setting, just somewhere you can focus.
>
> Take a few deep breaths. Feel your body in the present moment. Notice how your feet are grounded to the floor, your body's weight, the way your breath moves through your chest and belly. This helps bring you into the here and now.
>
> Allow yourself to feel whatever emotions are coming up. Acknowledge that there's a crisis happening. You're not trying to avoid the situation or the feelings; instead, you're simply recognizing them without judgment.
>
> Now become an observer of your own thoughts and emotions. Picture yourself stepping back and watching the crisis unfold, as though you're a neutral third party. You may imagine this like watching a movie of your own life, where you're not actively involved in the plot but just a witness to the events happening.
>
> Notice your emotions without identifying with them. For example, instead of saying, 'I am anxious,' observe the feeling: 'There is anxiety here.' This creates a space between you and the emotion, allowing you to detach from it.

As the observer, ask yourself these questions:

'What is happening right now?' (Focus on the facts, without emotional interpretation.)

'How do I feel about it?' (Recognize and label your feelings.)

'Is this something I can control right now?' (Detach from what's beyond your control.)

'What is the next best step for me to take, given the situation?' (Shift your focus to constructive action.)

Remind yourself that crises, like all experiences, are temporary. Nothing is permanent. Allow this to be a comfort; even if things are tough right now, they will shift over time. Repeat to yourself:

'This too shall pass.'

Think about what you're holding onto. Is it a particular outcome, an expectation, or a certain way things should go? Gently release that attachment, recognizing that you cannot force things to unfold a certain way. Trust that you'll navigate the situation with resilience, regardless of the outcome. To do this, you may want to step into the detachment ritual above (see page 237).

Gently return to the present moment. Notice how you feel now compared to how you felt before the exercise. Are you a bit more detached or peaceful? Even if it's only a small shift, celebrate it.

In times of crisis, the key is consistency. Try to practise this observer exercise daily, even if it's for just a few minutes, to help you strengthen the muscle of detachment. Over time, you'll find that you're able to step back more easily in challenging situations.

Doing the Work

Self-love is not just an idea – it's the relationship 'work' you do every day. It requires you to show up for yourself, especially when doing so feels difficult or uncomfortable. But it is in doing this solo work that you align with the energy of your Twin Flame Journey. This is the work that makes the difference between settling for a relationship that drains you and being able to recognize when a love is aligned with your soul's purpose.

Here are some more essential reminders to help you keep on doing the self-loving 'work' every single day, whether you are in a relationship or not:

Be Honest with Yourself

Self-love requires radical honesty. Ask yourself:

> 'What part of me still seeks validation outside of myself?'
>
> 'Where am I not honouring my own needs?'
>
> 'What am I avoiding in my life or in my relationships?'
>
> 'Where in my life am I sacrificing my own wellbeing for the sake of someone else's needs?'

Self-honesty is the starting point for transformation. Once you're clear about where you need to do the work, and grow stronger from the inside out, you can begin to take steps in a more self-loving direction.

Show Up for Yourself Every Day

If you want deep, unconditional love from a partner, don't ever stop giving that kind of higher love to yourself. Like energy seeks like energy. Think about the qualities you desire in a relationship – affection, kindness, respect and support. Are you offering these things to yourself? You cannot attract a love you are not willing to give yourself first. Begin to show up for yourself with the same care and compassion you would offer to your ideal partner. This is the work of becoming your own greatest supporter.

Another gentle reminder here that self-care is an essential part of healing from unrequited love. Take time to do practical things that bring you joy and fulfilment – whether that's creating art, travelling, beauty treatments or simply taking a relaxing bath. When you treat yourself with kindness and care, you reinforce the message that you deserve to be treated with love and respect.

Engage in activities that nourish your body, mind and spirit. Pursue hobbies or passions that make you feel alive. This is a time to reconnect with your own desires and dreams, independent of the love or validation you're seeking from another person. Self-care helps you create a strong foundation of self-love, which will make you more resilient and open to healthy relationships in the future.

Love Your Journey, No Matter How Long It Takes

The Twin Flame Journey is not a race – it's a process of personal growth, healing and alignment. It takes time. Think of yourself as the tortoise mindfully enjoying the journey and smelling the roses, rather than the hasty hare who runs out of steam. It is not about seeking perfection; it's about embracing your authentic self and allowing love to grow within you and flow to you naturally. The more you surrender to the process of self-love, the more effortlessly Cosmic Love will appear in your life. Remember, your Twin Flame is already on the way – but they can't show up until you are ready to receive them.

Relish the journey, knowing that everything is happening as it should. Instead of obsessing over the timing or wondering if your Twin Flame is out there somewhere, simply focus on being the best version of yourself and falling in love with the wonder of the present moment. When you finally stop desperately seeking love, you open the door for love to find you naturally. Just carry on doing the self-loving work every day and trust in your Twin Flame. Think of this work as pulling back the arrow in cupid's bow and carefully aiming you in the direction of your higher love. For the arrow to reach its target, there will come a time when you need to take a leap of faith and release it.

Know When and How to Let Go

Not all Divine Unions are meant to manifest in romantic union – whether immediately or ever. Sometimes, letting go is the most loving choice you can make, for yourself and for the other person. This is especially true if you feel that your emotional health is being compromised, or if the other person is consistently unavailable or unwilling to meet you halfway. Then, it is time to take a big step back.

Healthy Cosmic Love requires mutual effort. If both partners are willing to do the personal-growth work – facing their fears, healing old wounds, learning and growing together – and to support each other in the process, there's potential for a fulfilling union. But the opposite is true if you're constantly chasing someone who is emotionally unavailable, dismissive, or uncommitted even when you have honestly expressed how you feel. Love is not about trying to convince someone to love you. If your emotional needs are not being met and the other person is not interested in making changes, it is high time to honour yourself and move on.

Remember, your journey is about you first. Sometimes Twin Flames just need time to be apart from one another so they can work on themselves individually. And if both partners do the work, they can come back together in harmony.

A crucial milestone on your Twin Flame Path is learning when to let go of relationships that no longer serve your highest good. This can be one of the most challenging aspects of the journey, especially if you've invested your heart in someone who is unable to reciprocate. Sometimes, we hold on to relationships or feelings that are no longer aligned with our true selves, simply because we are afraid of being alone or afraid of change. But if you are truly on the path to meeting your Spiritual Mirror, you must be willing to release what no longer serves you – and that includes your fear of being alone.

Letting go does not mean giving up on love; it means releasing attachment to a specific outcome. It means trusting that your path will unfold as it should, without force or resistance. If you are uncertain whether to stay in or keep working on a relationship, here's how to know when to call it quits. A lot of the advice below has already been stressed, but the repetition is important here because it is easy to lose your head and misread the urgent signals from your heart when you are in a relationship that isn't working and you really want it to.

Notice the patterns. If you find yourself repeatedly chasing someone who isn't as invested as you, it's time to ask yourself why. What do you think you're missing? What void are you trying to fill? Recognizing these patterns will help you understand that sometimes the universe is gently nudging you away from something that isn't meant for you because it's not in alignment with your highest good. Trust that there's something better on the horizon.

I hate to break this to you but it is super important that I do. If you keep repeating the pattern of chasing people in relationships, or thinking you can fix them, or need to fix yourself to 'catch' them . . . If you are making all the effort and they are not reciprocating, even if they say all the right things . . . Their refusal to reveal to you, through their actions, that they are sincere and committed to you is *all the sign you need that it's time to let the relationship go*. You really need to be single until you can break that self-destructive pattern. You really need to take time out from dating and start figuring out how to make yourself happy and to heal independently.

Divine timing. If the person you feel you are in love with is not showing up in the way you need, perhaps that's because the universe has happier plans for you. Release your attachment to a specific timeline and allow the universe to guide you.

Do your self-love work. Switch the focus away from finding romance but keep your heart open to the possibility of your Twin manifesting in someone else too. Surrender to the universe and trust that it will happen however it happens. This is how you find peace. The emphasis should always be on your inner work, healing yourself and raising your vibration from the inside out.

Divine Unions do not follow the typical timeline of a relationship. They arrive when you are both ready for partnership. If the person you desire is causing you pain or disappointment, trust that they are either not ready or not aligned with your path. The universe will provide you with a new direction once you are open to it. Twin Flames come together at exactly the right moment – not a moment sooner.

Divine Unions are not always linear or immediate. The universe has its own timing, and sometimes it requires you to go through other painful love affairs to grow. Trust that everything is unfolding as it should, even if it doesn't look the way you expected. When you release the need to control the outcome and surrender to the process, you allow yourself to be open to new possibilities.

Have faith that when you are ready – emotionally, spiritually and mentally – you will attract the kind of love that aligns with your true self. Divine Unions are meant to happen when both souls are in alignment and prepared for the transformation that the union brings. Sometimes, that means taking a step back and focusing on your own growth first.

Surrender. True love cannot be forced. When you let go of control, you open the door for true love to enter your life naturally. Surrender the idea of forcing things to happen and instead allow them to flow as they should. If your Twin Flame Odyssey is not aligning with the person you are currently focused on, practise releasing control. Allow yourself the freedom to live your life fully, knowing that your Twin Flame will appear when the time is right – often in ways you haven't anticipated and when you least expect them to.

The End Is Your Beginning

Unrequited love isn't the end of your love story. Every relationship ending is an opportunity for a new beginning. The pain you feel is a catalyst for your personal and spiritual growth and the universe's way of guiding you back to look within yourself and find the love at the heart of you. Through this pain, you'll discover the power of loving yourself authentically, setting boundaries and letting go of what no longer serves you. In fact, it can be the beginning of something much more profound – an awakening to your own worth, your own power and your own ability to love. The pain you experience is temporary, but the growth and self-love that come from it are lasting.

The more you align with self-love, the more you will attract a Twin Flame who mirrors that love back to you. This journey is not about forcing love; it's about becoming the love that you long for and allowing everything else to flow from that place of inner wholeness.

Trust the process. Trust yourself. And, most importantly, trust that love will always find you – when you are ready to receive it, just as you are.

Your great love, your Divine Union, is out there; and to find it, you need to face parts of yourself that you are uncomfortable with and accept that it will not necessarily appear in the way you expected it to. To feel loved is to heal from feelings of lack and to discover, for yourself, that the best way to receive and experience love is from the inside out and then to live and become it.

When you learn to truly love yourself, you align with the energy of your Twin Flame whether they are in your life or not. And when that happens, a surefire sign that you are awakening spiritually and headed in the right direction for Cosmic Love is the activation of your psychic abilities. You begin to sense what is unseen and read the Twin Flame signs the universe is always sending. And from that moment on, nothing in this world or the next can separate you from the transformative, death-defying higher love that awaits you.

7

TWIN FLAME UNION AND YOUR AWAKENED PSYCHIC ABILITIES

The journey to Divine Union is the most intense and transformative experiences a person can undergo. It's not merely a love story; it's a psychic and spiritual awakening, an Ascension, that forces you to confront the deepest layers of your soul. To take back the missing parts of yourself and find oneness. And whether you are physically with your Spiritual Mirror or separated from them, this process of becoming whole from the inside out will lead to the activation of your innate psychic abilities.

This chapter will delve into the unbreakable connection between psychic and spiritual awakening on your journey to Divine Union and how it manifests within you. Along the way, it will offer some practical exercises and affirmations to help you harness and cultivate your inner psychic.

The Psychic and Spiritual Dimensions

To understand why you can expect your psychic abilities to awaken on your Twin Flame Journey, it's essential to remind yourself again and again of what you have learned in previous chapters – and that is the spiritual nature of the Divine Union. The concept of Twin Flames extends beyond the physical world; it is rooted in the idea that each soul has a perfect mirror. The Spiritual Mirror is not just a romantic partner; it is a mirror that reflects both your light and your shadow – and you can find that mirror in a relationship with someone else or within yourself. The energetic bond between Twin Flames transcends time, space and even physical separation. As such, when your Spiritual Mirror enters or exits your life, their energy creates shifts in your own, triggering an awakening of dormant abilities – including psychic potential.

It's not just about connecting with another person on a physical or emotional level. Cosmic Love is, at its core, the unification of dual aspects of your own being. It's the reunion of the masculine and feminine energies within yourself, the healing of your inner wounds and the rise to higher states of consciousness or bliss. As all these energies merge within you, they ignite the innate psychic faculties that are connected to higher realms of understanding.

For many on the path to Divine Union, psychic abilities emerge gradually and are deeply tied to emotional and spiritual evolution. Your ability to intuitively 'sense' your Twin Flame's energy or to receive messages from the universe often increases when you start to align with your true self. These gifts become a natural consequence of the healing and growth that takes place when you embark on your Twin Flame Journey as part of your spiritual Ascension.

The Activation of Psychic Abilities

Whether your connection with your Spiritual Mirror is physical or purely spiritual, as you grow in self-awareness, self-love and self-belief on your Twin Flame path you can expect a natural awakening of your psychic faculties. Why? Because sixth sense is in your spiritual DNA.

Your psychic ability is your innate potential to sense beyond your five senses of sight, hearing, touch, taste and smell. It is this psychic or intuitive part of you that knows what reason and logic suggest cannot be known and allows you to mentally travel beyond space and time. You can call this your consciousness or even your soul.

The word 'psychic' comes from 'psyche', meaning 'soul', or what is non-physical, unseen, infinite about you. It's a mysterious inner hunch – that vague knowing you can't explain but that is later verified. For example, you think of someone and they text you out of the blue shortly afterwards, or you have a gut instinct about someone or something that in time turns out to be true.

Everyone has an innate psychic ability. Whether you describe it as your intuition, sixth sense, gut instinct, precognition or your higher self, this is the part of you that is deeply sensitive and empathic and feels connected to everyone and everything. If you listen to it, it can offer you a wealth of wisdom about yourself, your relationships and your life. Remember, whenever your heart aches or you feel low or in need of validation from others, your inner psychic is calling your name. It is a loving sign that you are off track and need to redirect; that validation should come from the inside out, not the outside in.

Create a Psychic Shift Now

Your inner psychic is who you truly are. Your soul, for want of a better word. Placing your trust in externals – other people, the material world, possessions – to bring your love into your life can never make you feel loved. Your relationship with your inner psychic, or your inner world, is the source of all love and joy in your life; but sadly, many of us are programmed to look outside ourselves for what can only be found within. Indeed, we often spend more time cultivating our online persona than we do our inner psychic. Let's start redirecting all that self-diminishing energy right now.

Remember those heart-focused rituals in the early chapters of this book (see page 47)? Let's take you right back again to the beating of your heart. Focus on its steady beat now and celebrate the miracle of your existence and the fact that you can consciously choose your next thought and feeling and reaction. You are not a helpless bystander to the slings and arrows of outrageous fortune. You have inner strength and an inner world and when you make that simple inner shift you understand how transformative every moment of your life is. Simply asking yourself if you want to love and feel loved or feel unloved and empty can also create a mighty inner shift. Of course, you want to love and feel loved – and just recognizing how obvious your answer to this question is will immediately align you with your inner psychic and the Twin Flame direction you need to be headed in.

> It can initially feel scary to know that you have this choice and are responsible for choosing love and joy in your life, because you have been conditioned to ask others or to look outside yourself; but let go and have faith in your inner psychic to guide and inspire you. This doesn't mean you won't make mistakes again. You will inevitably make mistakes, as that is the only way you can learn. Experiment, love fiercely and hope rebelliously – and remember that on your Twin Flame Path the destination is the direction but not the goal. The goal is the journey and the adventure of living and loving your life, both the bliss of the highs and finding the inner strength and wisdom to rise like a phoenix from the lows.

The Sensitivity Scale

Everyone is born with an innate sixth sense or intuition but will discover and connect to that inner wisdom in their own unique way. Only around 20 per cent of the population have highly developed intuition, empathy and creativity and constantly sense what cannot be seen or explained. Those people often find the process of tuning into their psychic abilities more instinctive. The remaining 80 per cent are not a lost cause, though, as they can still experience moments of intense psychic awareness during times when their emotions are pushed to the surface.

Additionally, research with people who don't identify as highly sensitive (or who claim to have had no psychic experiences) shows that the parts of the brain associated with intuition, empathy and creativity wake up when they engage in daily meditation and other psychic-development tools for a couple of weeks.[5] Identifying as non-psychic may not represent the disadvantage you think it does, because the challenge for highly sensitive individuals is to set boundaries and filter out what is relevant from the endless invisible messages that come in. The challenge for people who are less naturally sensitive is to learn to open their psychic eyes in the first place, but the messages tend to be much clearer when they finally do so. In short, wherever you feel you are on the spectrum of sensitivity, your inner psychic is longing to connect with you and work with you.

How to Tune In

When you use your five physical senses, you are tuning into or reacting to the energy vibrations they create. Your psychic or sixth sense is different only in that it works with energies that can't be seen or rationally explained. And yet, every day, you believe in the reality of invisible forces you can't see or explain, such as electricity or sound waves or love. Psychic energy is similar. It is worth bearing in mind that *you* are unexplained energy too. Your very existence on this Earth is a mystery. Your psychic ability is just another part of that infinite mystery.

Your inner psychic is subtle and that is why many of us fail to notice it – or why, if we do notice it, we confuse it with an overactive imagination. However, the more you learn to tune into your inner psychic, the louder it will speak to you as you follow your Twin Flame Path. Like a muscle, the more you use it the stronger it becomes. That's why it is important to recognize how your inner psychic speaks to you. Most people think that psychic ability just happens to us – like a blinding light or disembodied voice. This is not untrue, but it is exceedingly rare; and in most cases it 'speaks' in extremely subtle ways that force you to look inwards and reflect deeply on your inner world. There are countless ways your psychic abilities can surface, but let's concentrate here on the four major categories that are most likely to emerge and help you find clarity on your Twin Flame Journey.

Clairvoyance (Clear Seeing)

Clairvoyance is the ability to see images, symbols, or visions, sometimes with your eyes open but mostly when they are closed. As you grow closer to your true self and allow the energies of your Spiritual Mirror to flow through you, you may experience sudden flashes of insight or images forming in your mind's eye. These mental visions, or visualizations, may relate to your current emotional state or future events and offer guidance about your spiritual journey. Some people experience clear Twin Flame visions in vivid dreams, while others may see symbols or images forming in their mind during meditation, or during routine activities like walking or showering that distract the conscious mind and offer space for psychic abilities to take centre stage.

If you think this sounds a lot like dreamwork and day-dreaming during the day, you would be correct there. Internal vision and nocturnal dreams are potentially psychic.

Twin Flame Clairvoyance Exercise

This exercise is designed to help you strengthen your clairvoyance. It can intensify your connection with and ability to sense your Spiritual Mirror's presence and messages about your Twin Flame Journey.

> Find a quiet space. Have a pen and paper handy. Close your eyes, take deep, heart-centred breaths and relax your body. Lightly massage the area in the middle of your forehead, which is believed to be your third or psychic eye.
>
> Visualize, describe to yourself or, on one side of a piece of paper, draw a picture of what your feel your inner energy or essence looks like. What shape or colour would it be? There are no rights or wrongs here.
>
> Then, visualize, describe to yourself or draw your Twin Flame's glowing energy alongside your own. Ask to connect your essence with their essence:
>
>> 'I invite the energy of my Twin Flame to show itself to me for clarity and love.'
>
> Focus on the area between your eyebrows (third eye). Imagine a soft indigo light there, enhancing your clairvoyance.

Visualize, describe to yourself or draw on another piece of paper your energy or essence upon uniting with your Twin Flame. What does that united energy look like? Make a conscious choice to see an uplifting image. Observe any sensations, thoughts, colours, or emotions that surface. Ask for any messages from your Twin Flame, then trust the insights or feelings you receive.

Slowly bring awareness back to your body, feeling grounded. Place your hands on the floor to anchor yourself. Write down any impressions, symbols, or feelings that come to you after the exercise.

By practising this exercise regularly, you'll naturally strengthen your clairvoyant abilities and develop a clearer, deeper Cosmic Love.

Observing the natural world around you can also help you boost your clairvoyant abilities. For example, you can do a spot of cloud watching. Lie down somewhere quiet and comfortable outside and look up at the sky. Then, notice how the clouds gently shift in the sky and what magical shapes they form and if those shapes speak to you in some way. Note down any significant thoughts that arise. You can do a similar practice while admiring the glorious colours of a sunrise or sunset, or by stargazing at night – these are all mesmerizing ways to develop your inner clairvoyant.

Clairaudience (Clear Hearing)

Clairaudience is the ability to hear inner messages from the spiritual realm, including from your Twin Flame. These may come through as inner voices or whispers in your mind, or words, phrases or songs that you can't get out of your head; you might even hear conversations during moments of stillness, meditation or deep telepathic connection. This can be particularly powerful when you are in physical separation from your Spiritual Mirror, as their energetic presence communicates their love for you across distance and time.

Twin Flame Clairaudience Exercise

This exercise is designed to help you enhance your clairaudience and intensify your connection with your Twin Flame. By focusing on listening to inner sounds and messages, you can strengthen your communication with your Spiritual Mirror on an energetic level.

Meditation encourages you to enter the state of receptiveness that is so conducive to hearing your inner voice and the voice of your Twin Flame.

Find a quiet space free of distractions. Close your eyes, take deep, heart-centred breaths, calm your mind and relax your body.

In your mind or out loud, call upon the energy of your Spiritual Mirror. Ask for clear, loving communication:

'I invite the energy of my Twin Flame and open myself to hear their messages.'

Focus on your inner ears, sensing them being gently tuned to receive clear messages of love and light. Gently massage with your fingers the area slightly above each of your ears, as this is believed to be your inner-ear chakra or spiritual-energy centre. Quiet your mind and listen intently, allowing any sounds, words, or impressions to come through. Pay attention to subtle tones, whispers, or phrases that feel connected to your Twin Flame. Don't force it. Simply allow your inner hearing to absorb any messages. Trust the sounds or words that come through, whether they're soft or clear. If nothing comes through, this may be a message reminding you of the power of silence and patience.

After receiving any messages, slowly bring your awareness back to your physical body. Place your hands on the floor to feel grounded and centred and drink a glass of water or have a light snack.

Write down any words, sounds, or impressions you received. Reflect on any guidance or messages from your Twin Flame. Regular practice helps deepen the connection.

Another wonderful way to boost your clear hearing is to listen to music that gives you goosebumps. Music can often act as the language of the soul. The much-loved 1994 movie

> *Shawshank Redemption* features a scene where the film's hero locks himself in a room and risks severe punishment to gift the inmates a few minutes of opera on the prison loudspeakers. This moment beautifully expresses the power of music. So, let more music that you love flow through you during the day and let your Spiritual Mirror know you are ready to hear them through the notes. You can also seek out a stream, river, lake or sea. Listen and wait to see if the water speaks to you – not through words, but through sounds and feelings. And if you ever get a chance to listen to a dawn chorus, birdsong is a delightful way to invite spiritual sounds and healing into your life.

Clairsentience (Clear Feeling)

Clairsentience involves the ability to sense or 'feel' the emotional or physical state of another person, often without them saying a word. It often manifests through your body in a gut feeling, or through a fluttering stomach, increased heart rate and so on. It is also heightened sensitivity to things you touch, taste and smell.

This is one of the most common energetic abilities that develop within Divine Unions. You may feel your Twin Flame's emotions, pain, joy, or confusion without them expressing it overtly. Similarly, you might feel the emotions of others in your environment more intensely. This heightened sensitivity to emotion allows you to connect deeply not only with your Twin Flame but also with the world around you.

Twin Flame Clairsentience Exercise

This exercise helps you develop your clairsentience, which is the ability to feel unseen energies and emotions. By focusing on the subtle messages your body and your emotions are always sending, you can sense the incoming presence of your Spiritual Mirror more clearly.

First thing in the morning, a few moments after waking, or last thing at night, just before falling asleep, when your mind is at its most impressionable, say out loud or with your thoughts:

'I invite the energy of my Twin Flame to connect with me, and I am open to feeling their presence in my body.'

First, focus your awareness on the energy centre that is your stomach and the messages it is sending you. You may want to gently cradle it with your hands. Repeat with your heart by placing your hand on it. What are your stomach and heart trying to tell you about your progress on your Twin Flame Path? You may feel warmth, tingling, or emotions that seem unfamiliar. Pay attention to any physical sensations or shifts in your mood.

Don't over-analyse – simply observe the physical sensations and feelings that surface alongside them. Trust any feelings of love, peace, or even discomfort, as

> these could carry psychic messages to help you on your Twin Flame Journey or even predict potential futures.
>
> Carry this heightened body awareness with you during the day. Regularly check in with your stomach, heart and the rest of your body too. Indeed, you could perform a mini body scan several times a day, sending love and gratitude to every part of your body. Notice what your body is trying to tell you or warn you about, as well as what your senses of taste, smell and touch want you to notice more deeply.

Intuitive Knowing (Claircognizance)

Claircognizance is the gift of 'just knowing' things without needing any logical explanation. This is a powerful psychic gift that often appears during moments of profound spiritual connection. You may suddenly know that your Twin Flame is thinking of you, or you may feel compelled to take certain actions that will lead you closer to union. When your higher self begins to align with your soul's purpose, your intuitive knowing becomes stronger and stronger as you move towards Divine Union.

> ### Twin Flame Claircognizance Exercise
>
> This exercise helps you develop claircognizance, a calm and clear sense of just knowing something to be real or true without needing to know why you know.

Find a quiet, comfortable space. Close your eyes, take deep, heart-centred breaths, calm and relax your body.

In your mind, invite the energy of your Twin Flame. Say to yourself:

> 'I invite the energy of my Twin Flame to connect with me through my inner knowing, and I open myself to receiving clear guidance.'

Focus on your crown chakra (top of your head), knowing that it is believed to be an energetic gateway to your higher wisdom and universal knowing. Gently pat the top of your head if it helps. Open your mind and allow any sudden insights or knowing to flow in. Trust that any thoughts or impressions that come to you are messages from your Spiritual Mirror, even if you don't fully understand them at the time. This could be a feeling of certainty, a thought, or a clear sense of something that appears without explanation.

Don't question the insights that flood in. Just allow the information to arrive and trust it. It may come as an instant knowledge, understanding, or a deep 'knowing' about your Twin Flame. If no insights come in, trust that is for a reason too and try again another day. The absence of insights is highly unlikely when you allow your mind and heart to open and channel the first information that comes in. The chances are that too much will crowd in, and your challenge will be to recall and decipher what came to mind first.

Slowly bring your awareness back to your body, feeling grounded and centred. Stand up, stretch tall and then perform a giant yawn with a battle cry.

Write down any sudden insights, thoughts, or impressions you received. Reflect on how these may relate to your Twin Flame and your journey and don't stress if they don't immediately make sense. Trust that in time they will and that the inner work is being done behind the scenes.

Practise regularly to strengthen this inner knowing. During the day, always pay attention to your first thoughts on meeting someone or in a new place. Keep a record of these thoughts and see how many of them come true and how many prove misguided. Try to establish what the conditions were for clear intuitive guidance so that you can replicate them.

Pick Your Own Psychic Channel

It is entirely possible that the more you focus on psychic awakening that you experience all four categories of psychic ability, as there is interchange between them; but you may also find that you are more in tune with one than the other. For example, your psychic insights could tend to be visual, in that you love to daydream and focus on dream recall. Or perhaps you often pick up vibes or feelings. Maybe you are receptive to sounds and music. Or do you just know things instinctively? Now you know that psychic awakening is integral to your Twin Flame Path, start to notice how your inner psychic prefers to speak to you and then focus your awareness on that psychic channel, rather than trying to force channels that don't feel as natural to you.

And in all your psychic-development work, take inspiration from your dreamwork; keep a record of any psychic impressions that came through and how they did so. Be sure to date them and revisit them every now and again with the benefit of hindsight, to see when your hunches were accurate and when they were not and try figure out why. You need to be your own Twin Flame detective, gathering your own proof that you are a psychic and spiritual being having a human experience.

And if you struggle to know the difference between your psychic senses and anxiety, psychic insight tends to be calm, clear and energizing. It will also encourage you to take proactive action. By contrast anxiety leaves you confused, conflicted and feeling drained.

The Psychic-Activation Process

Psychic activation during the Twin Flame Journey can occur at any time, but there are certain triggers that tend to amplify this process. These triggers can include emotional shifts, physical separation or reunion, deep inner healing and moments of spiritual awakening. Understanding the nature of these activations can help you recognize them as they arise.

Emotional intensity. The emotional waves that come with the highs and lows of the Twin Flame Journey – such as spiritual healing or relationships break-ups, grief, loss – can accelerate your psychic awakening. These shifts in emotion heighten your sensitivity to energy, which naturally triggers greater intuitive/psychic awareness.

Spiritual practices. Meditation, breathwork and other spiritual practices recommended in this book can all act as powerful catalysts for psychic development. When you engage in these practices with the intention of connecting with your higher self or your Spiritual Mirror, you activate areas in your brain associated with intuition, empathy and creativity and open a space for psychic abilities to flow through you.

Twin Flame separation and union. When you experience separation from your Twin Flame, whether physically or emotionally, the energetic shift is often intense. Paradoxically, the shock of this can lead to the activation of psychic abilities, as your soul searches for connection, meaning and healing. Similarly, reunions with your Spiritual Mirror can trigger a surge of energy that opens your psychic channels.

Inner union. Cosmic Love does not occur simply through the physical union of two people. It happens within the self. As you integrate and balance the conflicting energies within you, your psychic abilities may awaken as part of this inner healing and return to wholeness. The more you step into your higher self, and the more you align with your spiritual purpose, the stronger your psychic gifts will become on your Twin Flame Path.

Afterlife Signs

Once you become aware of the non-conscious nature of your inner psychic, the concept of there being an afterlife doesn't seem so inconceivable. As previously mentioned, given that quantum science suggests that everything is energy, and that energy is infinite and can't be destroyed, only transformed into something else, is it such a leap to think that the energy of your consciousness might survive bodily death?

The more you awaken spiritually and psychically, the more likely it is that you will believe in the possibility of an afterlife and the survival of your consciousness and the consciousness of those you love after death. You will just know that there is more to your life than the external or material and that there is fierce power in what is unseen. This is especially the case if you have experienced or are experiencing a Soul Mate or Twin Flame bereavement.

You may find yourself having dreams of your departed loved one and these dreams can offer you a comfort beyond understanding. You may also notice afterlife signs and synchronicities. For example, the inexplicable appearance of a white feather or a butterfly, the unusual behaviour of a bird – typically a robin or white owl, given their spiritual symbolism – or hearing a song that meant a great deal to your departed love at just the right time so it feels heaven-sent. Although feathers, butterflies, rainbows, coins, music and lost objects found are some of the most commonly reported afterlife signs, these signs can be quite literally anything that is deeply meaningful and reminds you that death ends a life and not a relationship.

The most powerful way to connect to a departed loved one is not to visit a medium but to think of them and talk to them with feelings of unconditional love. You can also meet them in your dreams. In some cultures, dreams are believed to be a portal between this life and the next. At the end of the day, it is a matter of your personal belief.

When people tell me they have not received a sign from their departed loved one, I ask them if they have dreamed of them or if they might want to consider incubating a dream about them. Research shows that afterlife dreams can significantly ease the grieving process – and to my mind that again is heaven-sent.

Incubating an Afterlife Dream

This exercise helps you set the intention to connect with a departed loved one through your dreams. By focusing your mind and creating a calm space, you invite their presence into your dream world.

When you place your head on your pillow at night, take slow, deep, heart-centred breaths. Relax your body, calm your mind. Silently affirm:

> 'I invite the spirit of [their name] to visit me in my dreams tonight.'

> To strengthen your intention, recall a specific peaceful, happy or loving memory or feeling associated with them and keep focusing on that memory until you fall asleep.
>
> Upon waking, immediately jot down any dreams or impressions, whether they featured your departed loved one or not. Even subtle feelings or symbols may carry meanings from the other side.
>
> By setting a clear intention and relaxing into the process, you invite your departed loved one into your dreams. Regular practice can deepen this connection over time; it may not happen overnight. But if your departed loved one does not in time appear in your dream, don't take this as a sign that they are not reaching out to you in spirit. They are, but for whatever reason dreams are not the way they choose to do so. They may prefer to meet you in your memories of them, your daydreams, in afterlife signs, in nature, in music and always in your heart.

Psychic Gifts as Preparation for Divine Union

The awakening of your psychic abilities is a mighty powerful tool on your journey to Divine Union, but it requires cultivation and care. Here are some further practices to help you nurture your psychic gifts and see the world within and around you with angel eyes.

Ground yourself regularly. Grounding is essential when developing your latent psychic abilities. Without grounding, you risk becoming overwhelmed by the energy you're receiving, making it harder to discern what is yours and what belongs to others. Regular grounding practices – such as walking barefoot on natural surfaces, practising mindfulness, or simply sitting quietly conscious of your feet on the ground – will help you stay connected to your physical body and maintain clarity in your psychic experiences.

Strengthen your inner voice. Your intuition is the foundation of your psychic abilities. Begin by practising trust in your inner voice. When you feel an intuitive hunch, whether it's about your Twin Flame or any other aspect of your life, pause and take a moment to listen to it. Journal about your intuitive experiences and compare them to the outcomes. Your confidence in your psychic abilities will grow as you track your intuition's accuracy and notice how it is more often right than wrong.

Meditate on your third eye. The third eye, located in the middle of your forehead, is believed in metaphysical circles to be the seat of clairvoyance, psychic knowing and spiritual insight. To activate this centre, sit in a quiet space, focus on your breath and think about a ball of light in the centre of your forehead. Imagine this light growing brighter with each breath, illuminating your psychic vision. If it helps to do so, gently rub the middle of your forehead with your fingers to activate it. Set the intention to open your third eye and receive guidance related to your Twin Flame Journey. And then, to protect yourself or if you feel overwhelmed, imagine that eye closing.

Protect your energy. As you open to psychic experiences, it's essential to protect your energy so you don't take on from others what is not yours. Imagine a shield of white or golden light surrounding you whenever you engage in psychic practices. This will help prevent outside energies from influencing your own. You can also carry protective crystals such as black tourmaline or selenite to maintain your energetic boundaries.

Go with the Flow

The path to Divine Union and the development of your psychic abilities is not linear. There will be moments of doubt, confusion and frustration, but that is all part of the learning and growing process. Each step you take, no matter how small, brings you closer to your highest self and your Spiritual Mirror. Affirmations like the ones below can help empower you from the outside in and the inside out. Open your mind and say them out loud or with your thoughts, suspending disbelief and feeling their power flowing through you.

> 'I trust and honour my intuition, my sixth sense.'
> 'My psychic abilities are awakening.'
> 'I can receive messages from my Twin Flame at any time.'
> 'I am grounded, protected and clear in my psychic practice and my path to unconditional love.'

'My heart and mind are always open to higher wisdom, guidance and Twin Flame love.'

The Love That Won't Hurt You No More

Whether you are in a Divine Union or in the process of inner union, rest assured that developing your psychic abilities will always bring comfort and healing and guide you towards the higher love and deeper wisdom that is your destiny. But don't force it or overthink things. If you have been following all the advice in this book, your psychic abilities will be a natural by-product of your transformation or spiritual Ascension on your Twin Flame Path.

Your psychic gifts are not just self-help tools for navigating the world of unseen energy – they reflect your progress on the path to higher love. They mirror your ongoing transformation into your higher self or Divine Union and your ability to let go of mindsets that no longer serve you. The previous chapter explored the profound anguish of unrequited love, but perhaps the hardest break-up of all is letting go of your past or past versions of yourself. If you can master the art of compassionate detachment from what no longer serves or inspires you, with the help of your open mind, your ever-watchful heart and your undying sixth sense, a miracle will happen. You will no longer feel any need to chase unconditional love, because you will embody it.

First Look

For a sneak preview of just how liberating and blissful it feels to embody love, please set aside a moment or two today to perform this penultimate heart-centred exercise before you digest the concluding reflections in this book. This exercise is the one that everything you have encountered, are encountering and will encounter on your Twin Flame Path have always been nudging you towards.

Putting Your 'I' into Love

This is a spiritual book, not a religious one; but whatever your religion or belief, the chances are that you are familiar with these famous verses from I Corinthians 13:4–7 because they are so often used in wedding vows.

> 'Love is patient, love is kind. It does not envy, it does not boast, it is not proud. It is not rude, it is not self-seeking, it is not easily angered, it keeps no record of wrongs. Love does not delight in evil but rejoices with the truth. It always protects, always trusts, always hopes, always preserves.'

But how much more personal and relevant these verses become if you substitute the word 'I' with the word 'love'. Find somewhere quiet where you won't be disturbed and read the following out loud. Notice how it makes you feel.

> 'I am patient, I am kind. I do not envy, I do not boast, I am not proud. I am not rude, I am not self-seeking,

> I am not easily angered, I keep no record of wrongs. I do not delight in evil but rejoice with the truth. I always protect, always trust, always hope, always preserve.'

And to take things even higher – from the unconditional love within you to the unconditional love all around and waiting to unite with you – try reading this out loud too.

> 'My Twin Flame is patient, my Twin Flame is kind. My Twin Flame does not envy, they do not boast, they are not proud. They are not rude, they are not self-seeking, they are not easily angered, they keep no record of wrongs. My Twin Flame does not delight in evil but rejoices with the truth. My Twin Flame always protects, always trusts, always hopes, always preserves.'

Conclusion
HIGHER LOVE

Always be prepared for your Twin Flame – you never know when they might find you, or how they will open your heart wide to the power of unconditional love for yourself, for them and for everyone and everything.

If you aren't loving your own company, why would you expect anyone else to?

So, if you are not currently with your Spiritual Mirror, just keep on elevating your self-love to attract them to you and spread the healing power of unconditional love to all those lucky enough to cross your path. If you can't physically see or touch your Twin Flame, there may well be times on your Twin Flame Journey that you doubt their existence. That is human. That is normal. Other people may tell you that true love exists only in the movies, or that signs and synchronicities are nonsense. Let them have their perspective, but remember that your perspective is your reality – and that the knowledge you now have from reading this book means you understand there is more to life than meets the eye. You know that there is love within your heart and that love is real and infinite and eager to return to you.

Your Twin Flame Path is really about your faith in the healing power of love. Learning to doubt yourself less and to trust yourself and the love that exists in your heart more. Because love really is the reason for everything. Everything that happens to us, especially the hard stuff, is a challenge to transform trauma into triumph, heartbreak into healing. And every time we succeed in doing that, our soul evolves and the force of light grows stronger than the force of darkness. You see, your Twin Flame Journey towards unconditional love isn't just about you finding your Spiritual Mirror. It is playing its part in raising collective consciousness.

Heart-Centred Ritual: Road to Compassion

This journey began by reintroducing you to the power of your own heart and it is only fitting that it should close in the same way, but knowing the beginning of this journey for the first time or seeing it from a higher perspective.

You will know when your heart is truly at peace and filled with love because it will naturally feel compassion for others and the planet. Compassion is born from the experience of tough and painful things. Through these experiences, we learn the power of being kind not just to ourselves but to others too. Your closing ritual in this book will help you nurture and grow the seeds of loving compassion and kindness. Take note of how performing this ritual makes you feel, as this will be a strong indicator of whether you are heading in the right direction on your Twin Flame Path.

> Find somewhere quiet where you won't be disturbed. Place your hand on your heart and breathe in and out deeply. Say out loud or with your thoughts:
>
> 'I am loved. I am at peace.'
>
> Then think of someone you care about and say out loud or with your thoughts:
>
> 'May you be loved. May you know peace.'
>
> Then repeat for someone you know but are not close to. Then repeat it for someone you are not close to or don't have a good relationship with. Finally, repeat it for everyone on the planet.
>
> 'May you all feel loved. May you all know peace.'

There has been a lot to reflect on, process and experiment within this book, so congratulations on reaching this point. Your commitment to your personal and spiritual growth on your Twin Flame Journey is outstanding and deserves recognition. But don't rest on your laurels. Your great love story is an ongoing process. The purpose of this concluding section is to offer a few new revelations but also, more significantly, to reiterate and reaffirm the seminal concepts you have explored so far. Some of this may feel repetitive but sometimes repetition is the best way to create the shift needed to transform love dreams into reality.

Think of it as your handy Twin Flame reference guide that you can revisit time and time again moving forward. If you feel you need deeper guidance and direction as you read this closing section, simply work through the previous chapters in the book again. I'm hoping that this cheat sheet – as you read it now and every time you re-read it, when you feel in need of a reminder and reassurance – will feel both familiar (in that your heart already knows what it will say) and constantly refreshing and surprising.

Rather like a great work of art, literature or a song you never tire of listening to because every time you listen you feel, sense or imagine something different or make new brainstorming connections, let the following reminders and revelations be your forever Twin Flame lighthouse.

Eternal Flame

The concept of Twin Flames is often depicted as the union of two souls – each mirroring and complementing the other in a deeply transformative bond. This bond can be romantic, but it can also be friendship or any relationship where there is intense love, respect, shared goals, philosophies, mannerisms and vibrations and a desire for mutual evolution that extends to improving humanity. There will also be an invisible magnetic pull between them that never goes away, even when the intensity becomes overwhelming and triggers physical separations. The spiritual nature of this bond means that this journey is just as much about union *within* yourself as it is about your relationship with another person. If you're not currently in a relationship with your Twin Flame, or you haven't yet met them, know that your journey is still in progress and that this time of separation is not wasted. In fact, it can be one of the most powerful and exciting phases of your path.

Whether you're seeking Cosmic Love with another person or focusing on the union within yourself, the essence of the journey is about psychic and spiritual awakening. Through this process, your Divine Union – both internal and external – can manifest according to its own divine timing.

Common Signs

Even if you're not yet in a relationship, the signs of your Twin Flame's presence will make themselves known. You may sense their presence energetically or they may manifest through intuitive hunches, synchronicities, repeating numbers or vivid dreams. All these are gentle reminders from the universe that your journey towards spiritual union is progressing and that the way forward is to continue to confront and heal aspects of yourself. But by far the most potent sign is that you begin to see beyond the material and your perspective shifts towards the spiritual meaning and purpose of your life.

A time for you. Before you can truly unite with another, you must first unite with yourself. The deeper the connection you have with your own heart, the more you will attract the union you desire with your Spiritual Mirror. It is important that you get to know yourself truly, madly and deeply. Practices like journalling, mindfulness, meditation, shadow and dreamwork will help you uncover what's waiting to be understood, forgiven, harmonized and healed within you.

Self-love. The more you love and accept yourself, the more you align with the energy of love that will naturally draw your Twin Flame to you. Take practical self-care steps. Start each day affirming your worth:

> 'I am worthy of love. I am deserving of deep connection. I love myself as I am.'

This will instantly help shift any negative self-talk and encourage a loving, positive inner dialogue. Taking care of your body, mind and spirit is an essential way to show yourself love. Whether it's through physical exercise, nourishing food, creative activities, time in nature or spending time with your pets and loved ones, make sure your daily life includes practices that nourish and uplift you.

And if you haven't already, please let go now of the idea that you need to be perfect to attract your Twin Flame. Don't condemn your flaws and imperfections – they are what make you human. Authenticity, not perfection, is what draws your Spiritual Mirror to you. Through those cracks the light comes in.

Find Your Purpose

Your Twin Flame is often tied to a higher mission greater than yourself. Even if you're not yet in a relationship, aligning with your own soul's purpose and exploring what you want to contribute to the world will raise your vibration and attract your Spiritual Mirror. So, seek out things every day that excite you and spark your creativity. What lights you up? Don't get trapped in the heartbreak of routine and the predictable. Whether it's art, writing, teaching, or healing, your soul's mission is an expression of your highest self. By focusing on your passions, on doing what you love, you elevate your energy, making you more magnetic to your Twin Flame. Whether it's helping others or working on self-development, make unconditional love and compassion for yourself and others your one true guide.

Trust

It can feel frustrating when you're not yet in union with your Twin Flame. However, the journey through separation is not only inevitable but necessary. This waiting period is about healing, growing and the incredible voyage of learning how to love yourself unconditionally. Stop chasing love and start attracting it with your self-love instead. The more you try to control the timing of your reunion, the more you block the flow of energy between you and your Spiritual Mirror. Trust that the universe has its own plan for when and how your union will manifest.

Use alone time for personal and spiritual growth. Confront your fears, get out of your comfort zone and heal your inner wounds. Each step of healing you take deepens your readiness for union. Remember those books and movies you love. If they had started with the happy ending, would they resonate so much? Think of *Harry Potter* without Voldemort or *Lord of the Rings* without Sauron. In simpler terms: a rollercoaster without the lows creating the highs. No. It is the journey, the growth, the loss and learning and the edge-of-your-seat unpredictable stuff that captivates, holds you spellbound, keeps you feeling alive.

It is the same with your Twin Flame Journey. It is all about finding the inner love, strength and wisdom you didn't know you had, often in the darkest places. You aren't going to find any magic or evolution or genuine love by staying in your comfort zone. Getting comfortable outside your comfort zone is the only way to go on your Twin Flame Odyssey.

Raise Your Vibration

Your vibration is your energetic frequency and it plays a key role in attracting everything you desire, including Divine Union. By raising your vibration, you align with higher states of being – love, abundance, peace and joy – which will make you more magnetic to love and happiness, whether within yourself or with another person. If you're not yet in a relationship, focusing on raising your vibration is one of the most transformative things you can do to prepare for the union.

Raising your vibration doesn't just mean thinking and feeling positive – it's about creating alignment between your body, mind, heart and spirit, and taking conscious action to uplift your energy. Here are some practical, holistic and healing vibrations-raising steps you can take every day on your Twin Flame Path.

Practical Ways to Raise Your Vibration

Meditation will help you find inner peace and reconnect to your higher self, so you can see the bigger picture. Dedicate five or so minutes a day to sit in a comfortable position and observe your thoughts without interacting with them. If you are new to the practice, you can find many guided meditations on YouTube or apps like Insight Timer or Calm. Look for meditations focusing on 'healing', 'Twin Flame connection', 'self-love', or 'raising your frequency'.

Gratitude is a high-vibration emotion that opens you up to more blessings. The more grateful you are, the more you magnetize love, abundance and higher vibrational experiences into your life – including your Divine Union. When you focus on what you have, instead of what you lack, your energy shifts from scarcity to abundance. Keep a daily gratitude journal. Each night, write down at least three things you're grateful for, whether they are small (like your morning coffee or a good book) or large (like your health, your family, or your dreams). This simple act trains your mind to focus on the positive, raising your vibration in the process.

Cleanse your energy regularly. Energy can get clogged or stagnant if you don't regularly clear it. Just like you clean your physical space, your energetic space needs cleansing to maintain high vibration. Negative emotions, toxic environments, or unhealthy relationships can weigh down your energy, preventing you from aligning with the Twin Flame frequency. One of the and simplest ways to cleanse your energy is to spend regular time in nature or green spaces. Walk barefoot on the earth, stand under a tree, or simply sit and breathe deeply as you connect with the natural world. You could also soak in a warm bath with Himalayan Sea salt or Epsom salt. As you relax, visualize the salt pulling out negative energy from your body and mind. Or you may prefer to burn sage or palo santo wood to clear negative energy. Move the smoke around your body, through your home and across your belongings to refresh the space.

What you eat affects your energy levels and overall vibration. High-vibration foods are those that are fresh, organic, plant-based and alive with nutrients. These foods help you feel energized, balanced and connected to your higher self. Eating heavy, processed, meat-heavy or artificial foods can lower your energy, making you feel sluggish and disconnected. Drink plenty of water, as hydration is key for maintaining high energy. Freshly squeezed juices or nutrient-packed smoothies are excellent for boosting your vibration. Try incorporating ingredients like kale, spinach, celery, lemon, ginger and apple as these help to detoxify your body, increase your vitality and keep your energy levels high.

Exercise is a powerful way to raise your vibration because it releases endorphins, clears stagnant energy and connects you to your body. The more you move, the more you elevate your mood and energy. Find a physical activity that you enjoy. Whether it's yoga, dancing, walking, swimming, or running, physical movement helps shake up any low-vibration energy and refreshes your system. Yoga is especially effective for aligning your energy centres and bringing balance to your body, mind and spirit. If your ability to move is limited for health reasons, find ways to work around that to the best of your ability. Sometimes simply sitting up and working on your posture or tapping your fingers can boost your holistic wellbeing, as can cold showers or washes and deeper breathing.

Breathing deeply through your nose rather than your mouth has an impact on your vibration. Try deep belly-breathing or nose-breathing techniques. These practices help you relax and raise your energy, especially if you're feeling stressed or anxious.

The people you spend time with, the environments you engage in and the media you consume all impact your vibration. Surround yourself with people who uplift you, places that make you feel calm and inspired and media that inspires positivity and growth. Evaluate the relationships and environments you are in. Are they supporting your highest good? Let go of toxic relationships that drain your energy and spend more time with people who encourage your growth and happiness. Consider joining communities or groups that share your spiritual or personal development interests, as this will help you raise your vibration through connection.

What you watch, read and listen to also influences your energy. Choose books, podcasts and movies that promote love, healing and personal growth. Limit exposure to negativity, whether it's through the news or certain social-media accounts. Fill your mind with positive, uplifting content to raise your vibration consistently.

Joy and laughter are among the highest-vibrational emotions. When you engage in activities that make you feel happy and carefree, you raise your frequency effortlessly. Do things that make you laugh and feel playful. Watch a funny movie, hang out with a friend who lifts your spirits, or engage in a hobby you love. Playfulness and a sense of fun are essential to maintaining a high vibration and connecting with your soul's true essence. If you're feeling stuck, try a laughing meditation or watching a comedy. Simply start laughing for no reason. This can feel silly at first, but laughter is infectious and soon your whole body will be infused with positive energy. It's an easy way to shift your vibration instantly.

Compassion and kindness not only raise your vibration but also create the energy of love that aligns you with your Twin Flame. When you are kind to others and practise empathy, you mirror the energy of love and abundance that you want to attract. Begin, of course, by offering kindness to yourself. Practise self-compassion by being gentle with yourself through difficult moments. Extend kindness to others, whether it's through a small act of generosity or simply offering a listening ear. As you practise kindness, you become more open-hearted and aligned with the energy of unconditional love. You also change the world for the better, one act of kindness at a time, as it has been shown that witnessing or hearing about kindness makes others more likely to perform acts of kindness themselves, creating a ripple effect that begins with amazing you.

The State of Your Divine Union

Raising your vibration and aligning with the energy of unconditional love is an essential part of preparing for your

Divine Union, whether that union is with yourself or with a partner. By focusing your energy on the practices above that elevate your energy – meditation, gratitude, healthy eating, physical movement and surrounding yourself with positivity – you align with the frequency of love, light and spiritual connection. The more you raise your vibration, the more magnetic you become to your Twin Flame. Then you realize that you don't need to take any classes or chant spells or invocations to attract them. These are engaging things to do, but they are not necessary. What is necessary is your understanding and trust that your Divine Union is a natural and magnetic one. It will happen when it is meant to happen. By doing the inner work, raising your frequency and cultivating love and peace within yourself, you naturally attract the relationship and union that is in alignment with your highest good.

As you continue your personal- and spiritual-growth work, know that your Twin Flame is on their own journey and that the universe will bring you together at the right time. Until then, focus on becoming the best version of yourself, living in alignment with your soul's purpose and embracing and expressing the love that is already flowing towards you. The union you seek is inevitable, and it all begins and ends with the union you create within.

You Are the Love You Seek

The union you seek with another is merely a reflection of the union you have already created within yourself. Use this blissful time, whether in separation or in preparation, to deepen your connection to your own soul. Heal, grow and align with your highest self, knowing that as you do, the universe is aligning everything for your perfect reunion – whether that's with your Twin Flame or your most authentic self.

And if you feel lost or make mistakes on your journey, remind yourself it is all part of the adventure. You need to lose yourself to find yourself on this Twin Flame Journey and gifting yourself a little time to wander on your Twin Flame Path is not a sign that you are lost; it just means you are taking time to savour the journey.

Never forget that Cosmic Love is not a destination but a continuous voyage of self-awareness, self-belief, love, growth and spiritual awakening. You are worthy of your Divine Union and it will manifest when the time is right, both within and outside of you. In the meantime, keep on shining your inner light and gratefully accept that, just as the sun will rise every morning and the moon will come out every night, the higher love you seek is already, always has been and always will be seeking the final destination that is you and only you.

'The course of true love never did run smooth.'
—*A Midsummer Night's Dream*

Source Notes

1. Wendy L Patrick, 'Why Couples Might Be More Likely to Break Up on Valentine's Day', *Psychology Today*, 16 January 2022 <https://www.psychologytoday.com/gb/blog/why-bad-looks-good/202201/why-couples-might-be-more-likely-to-break-up-on-valentines-day> [accessed 14 May 2025].
2. Arnie Seipal, 'The Dark Origins of Valentine's Day', *NPR*, 14 February 2022 <https://www.npr.org/2011/02/14/133693152/the-dark-origins-of-valentines-day> [accessed 14 May 2025].
3. 'The Science of Coherence', *HeartMath Institute*, 2025 <https://www.heartmath.org/heart-coherence/science/> [accessed 14 May 2025].
4. 'Retraining the Brain to Treat Chronic Pain', *National Institutes of Health*, 2 November 2021 <https://www.nih.gov/news-events/nih-research-matters/retraining-brain-treat-chronic-pain> [accessed 13 June 2025].
5. Cassandra Vieten, 'Extraordinary Experiences and Performance on Psi Tasks During and After Meditation Classes and Retreats', *IONS*, [n.d.] < https://noetic.org/research/extraordinary-experiences-and-performance-on-psi-tasks-during-and-after-meditation-classes-and-retreats/> [accessed 13 June 2025].

Acknowledgements

Sincere gratitude to my publishers Octopus for the inspiring books they publish, my editor Louisa Johnson for her vision, my agent Mark Gottlieb at TMG for his wisdom, and all the vibration-raising scientists, psychologists and experts I have worked with on my Twin Flame Journey and interviewed for my podcast, *White Shores*, and my weekly UK Health Radio show, *The Healing Power of Your Dreams*.

Heartfelt thanks to my family for their love, patience and support and my soul dog Arnie for forever healing my heart and my life.

And thank you from my soul to my readers and listeners. You are a never-ending source of love and joy and for that I am deeply grateful.

About the Author

Theresa Cheung is a modern mystic and *Sunday Times* bestselling dreams, personal- and spiritual-growth author, UK Health Radio show host and podcaster. She is a go-to expert contributor for TV, radio, podcasts and online and print media.

You can contact Theresa with any questions, stories or insights you want to share via her website (www.theresacheung.com), her email (angeltalk710@aol.com), Instagram (@thetheresacheung.com) or her author pages on Facebook and X.

Index

A
affirmations 74–5, 225–6, 236–7, 273–4
afterlife 39–41, 269–71
air signs (Gemini, Libra, Aquarius) 171
Akashic Records 190–2
anger, unresolved 68
anima and animus 62–3, 91–2
Aquarius 141, 177
    Aquarius rising 182
    Venus in 163–5
archetypes 63, 212
Aries 140, 174
    Aries rising 178–9
    Venus in 144–6
Aristotle 29
ascendant placement 177–82
ascension 134–5
astrology
    benefits of 138–9
    birth charts 139, 141–3
    elements 168–71
    North Node 173–7
    rising signs 177–82
    South Node 173–4
    sun signs 140–1
    Venus placements 143–68
    zodiac signs 140–1
    astrological placements 141–3
    Venus placement 143–68
bliss stage 122
boundaries, setting 227–9
breathing techniques 46, 287

B
behaviour patterns, recognising 246
bereavement 224–5, 269–71
birth charts 139

C
Cancer 140, 175
    Cancer rising 180
    Venus in 150–1
Cannon, Dolores 31
Capricorn 141, 176–7
    Capricorn rising 182
    Venus in 161–3
chakras 188
The Chariot (tarot) 184, 185
childhood. *see* inner child healing
clairaudience (clear hearing) 260–2
claircognizance (intuitive knowing) 264–6
clairsentience (clear feeling) 262–4
clairvoyance (clear seeing) 257–9
Clare, Elizabeth 31
co-dependency. *see* karmic relationships
coincidences 116–17
compassion 278–9, 288
conflict, dreams of 202–3
control, letting go of 248
cosmic love. *see* twin flames
crystals 194–6

D

déjà rêvé dreams 203–4
detachment 237–42
diet 286
divination. *see also* astrology
   Akashic Records 190–2
   crystals 194–6
   The Enneagram 189–90
   human design 188–9
   I Ching 188, 193
   numerology 117–18, 186–7
   the tarot 183–6
divine timing 247–8
divine unions. *see* twin flames
doubt stage 122
dream incubation 213–16, 270–1
dreams 117, 118, 204–5
   active imagination 214
   decoding 207, 209–12
   exercises 213–16
   importance of 199–200, 205–6, 217–18
   journalling 206–7, 213
   precognitive 203–4
   and psychic abilities 267
   recalling 206–11
   reframing 214
   symbolism of 200–4

E

earth signs (Taurus, Virgo, Capricorn) 170
the ego 125, 134–5, 210
elements in astrology 168–71
emotional manipulation 68
emotions
   clairsentience 262–4
   in dreams 209–10
   feeling 232–3
   and psychic awakening 267–8
   and the shadow 84–9
energy
   alignment with crystals 195
   cleansing 285–6
   protecting 273
The Enneagram 189–90
exercise 286

F

false flames 14–15, 77–90
   case study 82–3
   narcissists 84
   red flags 80–1
   and self-development 89–90
   shadow work 84–9
family members 109–12
film, twin flames in 3–4, 23, 39–40, 103, 104
fire signs (Aries, Leo, Sagittarius) 169
first impressions 177–82
The Fool (tarot) 184, 185
forgiveness 226–7

G

gaslighting. *see* false flames
Gemini 140, 175
   Gemini rising 179–80
   Venus in 148–9
gratitude 124, 285
grief 224–5, 232–3
grounding practices 46, 272. *see also* meditations
growth stage 123

H

healing and crystals 194–5
the heart
   alignment with 43–7
   healing with crystals 194–5
   and intuition 41–3
   reconnecting with 45–7
   rituals 47–56, 278–9
higher love 17–19, 39, 277–80
   journey towards 27, 32, 57
   and psychic awakening 268–9
honesty 7, 238, 242–3
human design 188–9

I

I Ching 188, 193
individuation 101, 211–12
inner child healing 67–8, 71–5, 211
inner union 268–9
integration 62–3, 97, 211–12, 268–9
intention setting 213
intuition 41–3, 255–6. *see also* psychic abilities
   claircognizance 264–6
   and crystals 195
   strengthening 272

J

journalling 86, 206–7, 213
Jung, Carl 62–3, 101, 211–12, 268–9

K

Kabbalah Tree of Life 188
karmic relationships 14–15, 65–7
   case study 68–71
   inner child healing 67–8, 71–5
   vs twin flames 75–6

L

labyrinths 51–3
Leo 140, 175
   Leo rising 180
   Venus in 151–3
Libra 140, 176
   Libra rising 181
   Venus in 155–7
literature, twin flames in 4–5, 30, 104
love. *see also* self-love; unrequited love
   changing perceptions of 115–16
   and grief 224–5
   and Venus placement 143–4, 167–8
love bombing. *see* false flames
The Lovers (tarot) 184, 185

M

mandalas 53–4
'masks'/'masking'. *see* the persona
meditations 87–9, 119–21, 272–3, 285
mindfulness practice 235
mythology, twin flames in 28–30
myths about twin flames 33–41

N

narcissists 84
North Node 173–7

numerology 117–18, 186–7
nurturing yourself 227

P
people-pleasing. *see* karmic relationships
the persona 91. *see also* rising signs
personality (Jung)
　anima and animus 62–3
　parts of 62–3, 90–1
　the shadow 82, 84–9
perspective, shifting 233–5
Pisces 141, 177
　Pisces rising 182
　Venus in 165–7
Plato 24–5, 28–9
platonic twin flames 107–9
precognitive dreams 203–4
psychic abilities 251–2, 274
　activation of 253–5, 267–9
　affirmations 273–4
　and afterlife signs 269–71
　nurturing 271–3
　sensitivity scale 255–6
　tuning in to 256–67
purpose 36, 116, 235–6, 283

R
reincarnation 31, 40, 67, 92
relationships 288. *see also* unrequited love
　boundaries in 227–9
　in dreams 210–11
　false flames 14–15, 77–90
　family members 110
　harmonizing 196
　importance of 11–13
　karmic 14–15, 65–76
　letting go of 63–5, 237–42, 244–8
　platonic 37, 39
　romantic 37, 39, 116
　and self-development 11–13, 61–2, 64
　soul mates 14–15, 37, 90–101
reunion stage 124
rising signs 177–82

S
Sagittarius 140, 176
　Sagittarius rising 181–2
　Venus in 159–61
Scorpio 140, 176
　Scorpio rising 181
　Venus in 157–9
the self 62, 212
self-awareness 82, 113, 138–9, 281
self-care 227, 243
self-development
　ascension 134–5
　inner child healing 67–8, 71–5
　and relationships 11–15, 61–2, 64, 76
　and search for twin flame 57
　shadow work 84–9
　and soul mates 37
　and twin flame 103–4, 105–6
self-forgiveness 226–7
self-love 5, 282, 289–90
　as antidote to false flames 82, 84
　and behaviour patterns 246
　and crystals 194

and honesty 242–3
importance of 6, 221–4
journey of 13–15, 33–4, 244, 278–80
practising 225–30, 233–49
and self-sufficiency 34–5
and sense of purpose 36, 116
and unrequited love 219–30
self-sufficiency 34–5, 62–3, 115, 221–2. *see also* integration
self-worth 225–6, 236–7
separation 123–4, 202–3, 268
sex, dreams of 203
the shadow 85–9
shadow work 82, 84–9, 203
solo twin flames 127–31
soul mates 14–15
benefits of 98–100
case study 92–3
the persona and anima/animus 91–2
reflection 95–6
and self-development 93–5
vs twin flames 37, 98–100, 126–7
South Node 173–4
spiritual growth 11–13, 32, 41–3, 251–2. *see also* higher love; relationships; self-love; the heart
spiritual mirrors. *see* twin flames
spiritual practices and psychic awakening 268
split souls (Plato) 28, 34
The Sun (tarot) 184, 185
sun signs 140–1. *see also* zodiac signs

surrender stage 124–5
synchronicities 116–17

T
the tarot 183–6
Taurus 140, 175
 Taurus rising 179
 Venus in 146–8
third eye meditation 272–3
trust 121–2, 283–4
twin flames 2, 3, 280–8. *see also* higher love
 attraction rituals 119–22
 case studies 106–7, 108–9
 family members 109–12
 and growth 103–6
 history of 24–5, 28–33
 meeting 23, 25–7, 35, 104–7, 122
 platonic 107–9
 in pop culture 4–5
 readiness for 118–19, 132–3
 search for vs attracting 38
 signs to look for 281–2
 solo twin flames 127–31
 stages of relationship 122–5
 vs karmic relationships 75–6
 vs soul mates 98–100, 126–7
 waiting for 112–18, 132–3
Two of Cups (tarot) 184, 185

U
unconditional love 23–4, 104–7, 124–5. *see also* higher love; twin flames
 ascension 134–5
 exercises 275–6

union with twin flame 202, 268
unrequited love 219–20
    benefits of 220–1, 231, 248–9
    case study 230–1
    moving through 231–42
    and self-love 221–30
    setting boundaries 227–9

V
Valentine's Day 6–11
Venus
    in air signs 171
    in earth signs 170
    in fire signs 169
    in water signs 172
Venus signs 143–68
vibration, raising 121, 134–5, 284–9

Virgo 140, 176
    Venus in 153–5
    Virgo rising 180–1

W
water signs (Cancer, Scorpio, Pisces) 172
The World (tarot) 184, 185

Y
yin-yang symbol 50–1

Z
zodiac signs 140–1
    and elements 168–71
    and North Node 174–7
    and Venus placement 143–68

Also by Theresa Cheung

Now available in hardback and eBook.

Also by Theresa Cheung

Now available in hardback and eBook.

RAISING READERS
Books Build Bright Futures

Dear Reader,

We'd love your attention for one more page to tell you about the crisis in children's reading, and what we can all do.

Studies have shown that reading for fun is the **single biggest predictor of a child's future life chances** – more than family circumstance, parents' educational background or income. It improves academic results, mental health, wealth, communication skills, ambition and happiness.[1]

The number of children reading for fun is in rapid decline. Young people have a lot of competition for their time. In 2024, 1 in 10 children and young people in the UK aged 5 to 18 did not own a single book at home.[2]

Hachette works extensively with schools, libraries and literacy charities, but here are some ways we can all raise more readers:

- Reading to children for just 10 minutes a day makes a difference
- Don't give up if children aren't regular readers – there will be books for them!
- Visit bookshops and libraries to get recommendations
- Encourage them to listen to audiobooks
- Support school libraries
- Give books as gifts

There's a lot more information about how to encourage children to read on our website: **www.RaisingReaders.co.uk**

Thank you for reading.

---

[1] OECD, '21st-Century Readers: Developing Literacy Skills in a Digital World', 2021, https://www.oecd.org/en/publications/21st-century-readers_a83d84cb-en.html

[2] National Literacy Trust, 'Book Ownership in 2024', November 2024. https://literacytrust.org.uk/research-services/research-reports/book-ownership-in-2024